WITHDRAWN

Creative
Resources

of Colors, Food, Plants, and Occupations

Creative
Resources

of Colors, Food, Plants, and Occupations

Judy Herr
Yvonne Libby

Delmar Publishers

I(T)P® International Thomson Publishing

Albany • Bonn • Boston • Cincinnati • Detroit • London • Madrid
Melbourne • Mexico City • New York • Pacific Grove • Paris • San Francisco
Singapore • Tokyo • Toronto • Washington

NOTICE TO THE READER

Publisher does not warrant or guarantee any of the products described herein or perform any independent analysis in connection with any of the product information contained herein. Publisher does not assume, and expressly disclaims, any obligation to obtain and include information other than that provided to it by the manufacturer.

The reader is expressly warned to consider and adopt all safety precautions that might be indicated by the activities described herein and to avoid all potential hazards. By following the instructions contained herein, the reader willingly assumes all risks in connection with such instructions.

The publisher makes no representations or warranties of any kind, including but not limited to, the warranties of fitness for particular purpose or merchantability, nor are any such representations implied with respect to the material set forth herein, and the publisher takes no responsibility with respect to such material. The publisher shall not be liable for any special, consequential or exemplary damages resulting, in whole or in part, from the readers' use of, or reliance upon, this material.

Cover Design by: Ron Sohn

Delmar Staff
Acquisitions Editor: Jay S. Whitney
Associate Editor: Erin O'Connor-Traylor
Developmental Editor: Ellen Smith
Project Editor: Karen Leet
Production Coordinator: Sandra Woods
Art & Design Coordinator: Carol Keohane

COPYRIGHT © 1998
By Delmar Publishers
a division of International Thomson Publishing Company

I(T)P® The ITP logo is a trademark under license.

Printed in the United States of America

For more information, contact:

Delmar Publishers
3 Columbia Circle Drive, Box 15015
Albany, New York 12212-5015

International Thomson Publishing
Berkshire House
168-173 High Holborn
London, WC1V7AA
England

Thomas Nelson Australia
102 Dodds Street
South Melbourne 3205
Victoria, Australia

Nelson Canada
1120 Birchmont Road
Scarborough, Ontario
M1K 5G4, Canada

International Thomson Publishing GmbH
Konigswinterer Str. 418
53227 Bonn
Germany

International Thomson Publishing Asia
221 Henderson Bldg. #05-10
Singapore 0315

International Thomson Publishing Japan
Hirakawacho Kyowa Building, 3F
2-2-1 Hirakawacho
Chiyoda-ku, Tokyo 102
Japan

International Thomson Editores
Campos Eliscos 385, Piso 7
col Polanco
11560 Mexico, DF Mexico

1 2 3 4 5 6 7 8 9 10 XXX 03 02 01 00 99 98 97

Library of Congress Cataloging-in-Publication Data

Herr, Judy.
    Creative resources of colors, food, plants, and occupations / Judy
Herr, Yvonne Libby.
        p.   cm.
    ISBN 0-7668-0017-2
    1. Education, Preschool—Curricula. 2. Creative activities and
seat work. 3. Unit method of teaching. 4. Color—Study and
teaching—Activity programs. 5. Food—Study and teaching—
Activity programs. 6. Plants—Study and teaching—Activity programs.
7. Occupations—Study and teaching—Activity programs. I. Libby,
Yvonne. II. Title.
LB1140.4.H486   1998
372.21—dc21   97-11205
                                                  CIP

CONTENTS

PREFACE

While reviewing early childhood curriculum resources, it becomes apparent that few books are available using a thematic or unit approach for teaching young children. As a result, our university students, colleagues, and alumni convinced us of the importance of such a book. Likewise, they convinced us of the contribution the book could make to early childhood teachers and, subsequently, to the lives of young children.

Before preparing the manuscript, we surveyed hundreds of child care, preschool, and kindergarten teachers. Specifically, we wanted them to share their curriculum problems and concerns. Our response has been to design and write a reference book tailored to their teaching needs using a thematic approach. Each theme or unit contains a flowchart, theme goals, concepts for the children to learn, theme-related vocabulary words, music, fingerplays, science, dramatic play, creative art experiences, sensory, mathematics, cooking experiences, and resources. Additionally, creative ideas for designing child-involvement bulletin boards and parent letters have been included. These resources were identified, by the teachers included in our survey, as being critical components that have been lacking in other curriculum guides.

In addition to the themes included in this book, others can be found in *Creative Resources of Art, Brushes, Buildings . . .* and *Creative Resources of Birds, Animals, Seasons, and Holidays.* More can and should be developed for teaching young children. The authors, however, wish to caution the readers that it is the teacher's responsibility to select, plan, and introduce developmentally appropriate themes and learning experiences for his group of children. Specifically, the teacher must tailor the curriculum to meet the individual needs of the children. Consequently, we encourage all teachers to carefully select, adapt, or change any of the activities in this book to meet the needs, abilities, and interests of their group of children to ensure developmental appropriateness. A handy reference for checking developmental norms is included on pages xiii and xiv.

As you use this guide, you will note that some themes readily lend themselves to particular curriculum areas. As a result, the number of activities listed under each curriculum area will vary from theme to theme.

The detailed Introduction that follows is designed to help teachers use the book most effectively. It includes:

1. a discussion on how to develop the curriculum using a thematic approach;
2. a list of possible themes;
3. suggestions for writing parent letters;
4. methods for constructing and evaluating creative involvement bulletin boards; and
5. criteria for selecting children's books.

This book would not have been possible without the constant encouragement provided by our families, the laboratory teachers in the Child and Family Study Center, and the faculty, students, and alumni of the University of Wisconsin-Stout. Our thanks to all of these people and especially to Carla Ahmann, Susan Babler, Mary Babula, Terry Bloomberg, Margaret Braun, Renee Bruce, Anne Budde, Michelle Case, Jill Church, Bruce Cunningham, Jeanette Daines, Carol Davenport, Jill Davis, Mary DeJardin, Linda DeMoe, Rita Devery, Donna Dixon, Esther Fahm, Lisa Fuerst, Shirley Gebhart, Judy Gifford, Nancy Graese, Barbara Grundleger, Betty Herman, Patti Herman, John Herr, Mark Herr, Joan Herwig, Carol Hillmer, Priscilla Huffman, Margy Ingram, Paula Iverson, Angela Kaiser, Elizabeth (Betz) Kaster, Trudy King, Leslie Koepke, Beth Libby, Janet Maffet, Marian Marion, Janet Massa, Nancy McCarthy, Julie Meyers, Betty Misselt, Teresa Mitchell, Kathy Mueller, LaVonne Mueller, Robin Muza, Paula Noll, Sue Paulson, Mary Pugmire, Kelli Railton, Lori Register, Peg Saienga, Kathy Schaeffer, Mary Selkey, Cheryl Smith, Sue Smith, Amy Sprengler, Karen Stephens, Barbara Suihkonen, Judy Teske, Penny Warner, Connie Weber, Ed Wenzell, Mary Eileen Zenk, and Karen Zimmerman. We are also grateful to our reviewers: Gerri A. Carey, McLennan Community College, Waco, TX; Billie Coffman, PA College of Technology, Williamsport, PA; Ione Garcia, IL State University, Normal, IL; Ned Sauls, Wayne Community College, Goldsboro, NC; and Becky Wyatt, Murray State College, Tishomingo, OK. Finally, our special thanks to two individuals whose assistance made this book possible. Jay Whitney, our editor from Delmar, provided continous encouragement, support, and creative suggestions. Also, special thanks to Robin Muza, our typist and research assistant.

INTRODUCTION

The purpose of this introduction is to explain the process involved in curriculum planning for young children using the thematic, or unit approach. To support each theme, planning and construction ideas are included for bulletin boards, parent letters, and a wide variety of classroom learning experiences.

Curriculum Planning

As you use this guide, remember that children learn best when they can control and act upon their environment. Many opportunities should be available for seeing, touching, tasting, learning, and self-expression. Children need hands-on activities and choices. To construct knowledge, children need to actively manipulate their environment. To provide these opportunities, the teacher's primary role is to set the stage by offering many experiences that stimulate the children's senses and curiosity; children learn by doing and play is their work. As a result, it is the authors' intention that this book will be used as a resource. Specifically, the ideas in this book should help you to enrich, organize, and structure the children's environment, providing them an opportunity to make choices among a wide variety of activities that stimulate their natural curiosity. Knowledge of child development and curriculum must be interwoven. To illustrate, play in the classroom should be child-centered and self-initiated. To provide an environment that promotes these types of play, it is the teacher's role to provide unstructured time, space, and materials. Using a theme approach to plan curriculum is one way to ensure that a wide variety of classroom experiences are provided. Successful early childhood programs provide interesting, challenging, and engaging environments. Children need to learn to think, reason, and become decision makers.

It is important that all curricula be adapted to match the developmental needs of children at a particular age or stage of development. An activity that is appropriate for one group of children may be inappropriate for another. To develop an appropriate curriculum, knowledge of the typical development of children is needed. For this reason, the section following this Introduction contains such information. Review these developmental norms before selecting a theme or specific activities.

Theme Planning

A developmentally appropriate curriculum for young children integrates the children's needs, interests, and abilities and focuses on the whole child. Cognitive, social, emotional, and physical development are all included. Before planning curriculum, observe the children's development. Record notes of what you see. At the same time, note the children's interests and listen carefully. Children's conversations provide clues; this information is vital in theme selection. After this, review your observations by discussing them with other staff members. An appropriate curriculum for young children cannot be planned without understanding their development and interests.

There are many methods for planning a curriculum other than using themes. In fact, you may prefer not to use a theme during parts of the year. If this is your choice, you may wish to use the book as a source of ideas, integrating activities and experiences from a variety of the themes outlined in the book.

Planning a curriculum using a theme approach involves several steps. The first step involves selecting a theme that is appropriate for the developmental level and interests of your group of children. Themes based on the children's interests provide intrinsic motivation for exploration and learning. Meaningful experiences are more easily comprehended and remembered. Moreover, curiosity, enjoyment of participation, and self-direction are heightened. After selecting a theme, the next step is developing a flowchart. From the flowchart, goals, conceptual understandings, and vocabulary words can easily be extracted. The final step in curriculum planning is selecting activities based upon the children's stages of development and available resources. While doing this, refer to pages xiii and xiv, Developmental Benchmarks, to review development characteristics for children of different ages.

To help you understand the theme approach to curriculum development, each step of the process will be discussed. Included are assessing the children's needs, and developing flowcharts, theme goals, concepts, vocabulary, and activities. In addition, suggestions are given for writing parent letters, designing bulletin boards, and selecting children's books.

Assessment

Assessment is important for planning curriculum, identifying children with special needs, and communicating a child's progress to parents. Assessment needs to be a continuous process. It involves a process of observing children during activities throughout the day, recording their behaviors, and documenting their work. Assessment involves records and descriptions of what you observe while the behavior is occurring. Logs and journals can be developed. The developmental norms that follow this Introduction can be used as a checklist of behavior. You can create a profile of the children's individualized progress in developing skills. Your observations should tell what the children like, don't like, have discovered, know, and want to learn.

Samples of the children's work in an individual portfolio collection should be maintained. A portfolio documents the children's progress, achievements, and efforts. Included should be samples of the children's paintings, drawings, storytelling experiences, oral and written language. Thus, the portfolio will include products and evidence of the children's accomplishments.

By reviewing the assessment materials you can deduce the children's developmental needs and interests. This information will be important in selecting a theme that interests the children and in selecting developmentally appropriate learning experiences.

Flowcharts/Webbings. The flowchart is a simple way to record all possible subconcepts that relate to the major concept or theme. To illustrate, plan a theme on apples. In the center of a piece of paper, write the word "apple." Then using an encyclopedia as a resource, record the subconcepts that are related. Include origin, parts, colors, tastes, sizes, textures, food preparation, and nutrition. The flowchart on page ix includes these concepts. In addition, under each subconcept, list content that could be included. For example, apples may be colored green, yellow, or red. By using a thematic approach, we teach children the way environments and humans interconnect. This process helps children make sense out of the human experience.

Theme Goals. Once you have prepared a flowchart webbing, abstracting the theme goals is a simple process. Begin by reviewing the chart. Notice the subheadings listed. For the unit on apples, the subheadings include: foods, parts, forms, and colors. Writing each of these subheadings as a goal is the next step of the process.

Since there were four subheadings, each of these can be included as a goal. In some cases, subheadings may be combined. For example, note the fourth goal listed. It combines several subheadings.

Through participation in the experiences provided by using apples as a curriculum theme, the children may learn:

1. Parts of an apple.
2. Preparation of apples for eating.
3. Apple tastes.
4. Textures, sizes, and colors of apples.
5. The origin of an apple.

Concepts. The concepts must be related to the goal; however, they are more specific. To write the concepts, study the goals. Then prepare sentences that are written in a simple form that children can understand. Examples of concepts for a unit on apples may include:

1. An apple is a fruit.
2. An apple has five parts: seed, core, meat, skin, and stem.
3. Apples grow on trees.
4. A group of apple trees is called an orchard.
5. Bread, pies, puddings, applesauce, dumplings, butter, and jellies can be prepared from apples.
6. Some apples are sweet; others are sour.
7. Apples can be colored green, yellow, or red.
8. Apples can be large or small.
9. Apples can be hard or soft.
10. Apples can be eaten raw.
11. Seeds from an apple can grow into a tree.

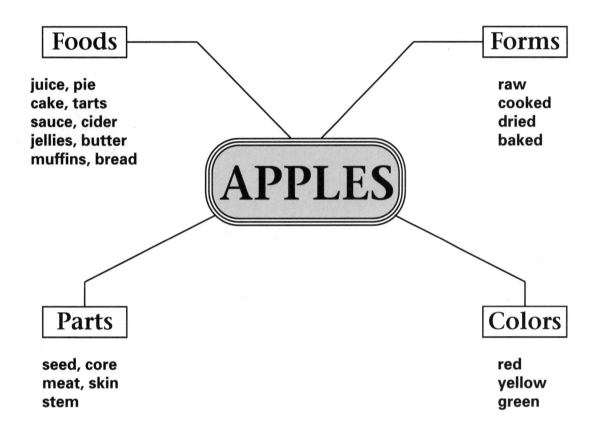

Foods

juice, pie
cake, tarts
sauce, cider
jellies, butter
muffins, bread

Forms

raw
cooked
dried
baked

APPLES

Parts

seed, core
meat, skin
stem

Colors

red
yellow
green

Vocabulary. The vocabulary should include new words that you want to informally introduce to the children. Vocabulary words need to be tailored to meet the specific needs of your group of children. The number of vocabulary words will vary, depending upon the theme and the developmental level of the children. For example, it might be assumed that the children know the word sweet, but not tart. So, the definition of the word tart is included. Collectively, the following words could be introduced in this unit: apple, texture, core, blossom, and apple butter. Definitions for these words could include:

1. apple—a fruit that is grown on a tree.
2. texture—how something feels.
3. core—the part of the apple that contains the seeds.
4. apple blossom—a flower on the apple tree.
5. apple butter—a spread for bread made from apples.

Activities. Now that you have learned how to develop goals related to a theme using a flowchart, you will need to learn how to select developmentally appropriate activities. You will find that many theme goals can be accomplished by additions to the environment, bulletin boards, field trips, and stories or resource people at group time. Your major role as an adult, or teacher, is that of a facilitator, planning and preparing the environment to stimulate the child's natural curiosity.

To begin this process, review each goal and determine how it can be introduced in the classroom. For example, if you were going to develop a theme on apples, review the goals. A bulletin board or game could introduce the three colors of apples. The children could also learn these colors through cooking experiences. The third vehicle for teaching the colors of apples would be placing the three colors of apples on a science table.

The five parts of an apple could also be introduced through participation in a tasting or cooking experience, bulletin board, or even discussion on a field trip or at the snack table. Always remember that children need to observe and manipulate the concrete object while engaged in child-initiated or child-directed play that is teacher supported. For that reason, fresh apples could be cut horizontally and placed on the science table with a magnifying glass. Likewise, simultaneously, apple seeds and paper could be available on the art table to construct a collage. Always remember that the best activities for young children are hands-on and open-ended. That is: focus on the process, rather than the product. Children need to learn to think, reason, and become problem solvers. As a teacher, you should take the ideas in this book and use and adapt them for planning and preparing the environment. Always remember that successful early childhood programs provide interesting, challenging, and engaging environments.

Parent Letters

Communication between the child's home and school is important. It builds mutual understanding and cooperation. With the efficiency of modern technology, parent letters are a form of written communication that can be shared on a weekly basis. The most interesting parent letters are written in the active voice. They state that the subject did something. To illustrate, "Mark played with blocks and read books today."

When writing the parent letter, consider the parent's educational level. Then write the letter in a clear, friendly, concise style. To do this, eliminate all words that are not needed. Limit the length of the letter to a page or two. To assist you with the process, an example of a parent letter is included for each theme.

Parent letters can be divided into three sections. Included should be a general introduction, school activities, and home activities. One way to begin the letter is by introducing new children or staff, or sharing something that happened the previous week. After this, introduce the theme for the coming week by explaining why it was chosen.

The second section of the parent letter could include some of the goals and special activities for the theme. Share with the parents all of the interesting things you will be doing at school throughout the week. By having this information, parents can initiate verbal interaction with their child.

The third section of the parent letter should be related to home activities. Suggest developmentally appropriate activities that the parents can provide in the home. These activities may or may not relate to the theme. Include the words of new songs and fingerplays. This section can also be used to provide parenting information such as the developmental value of specific activities for young children.

Bulletin Boards

Bulletin boards add color, decoration, and interest to the classroom. They also communicate what is happening in the classroom to parents and other visitors. The most effective bulletin boards involve the child. That is, the child will manipulate some pieces of the board. As a result, they are called involvement bulletin boards. Through the concrete experience of interacting with the bulletin board materials, children learn a variety of concepts and skills. Included may be size, shape, color, visual discrimination, eye-hand coordination, etc.

Carefully study the bulletin boards included for each theme in this book. They are simple, containing a replica of objects from the child's immediate environment. Each bulletin board has a purpose. It teaches a skill or concept.

As you prepare the bulletin boards provided in this book, you will become more creative. Gradually, you will combine ideas from several bulletin boards as you develop new themes for curriculum.

An opaque projector is a useful tool for individuals who feel uncomfortable with their drawing skills. Using the opaque projector, you can enlarge images from storybooks, coloring books, greeting cards, wrapping paper, etc. To do this, simply place the image to be copied in the projector. Then tape paper or tagboard on the wall. Turn on the projector. Using a pencil, color marker or crayon, trace the outline of the image onto the paper or tagboard.

Another useful tool for preparing bulletin boards is the overhead projector. Place a clear sheet of acetate on the picture desired for enlargement. This may include figures from a coloring book or storybook. Trace around the image using a washable marker designed for transparencies. Project the image onto a wall and follow the same procedures as with the opaque projector.

To make your bulletin board pieces more durable, laminate them. If your center does not have a laminating machine, use clear contact paper. This process works just as well, but it can be more expensive.

Finally, the materials you choose to use on a bulletin board should be safe and durable. Careful attention should be given when selecting attachments. For two-, three- and four-year-old children, adhesive velcro and staples are preferred attachments. Push pins may be used with older children under careful supervision.

Selecting Books

Books for young children need to be selected with care. Before selecting books, once again, refer to the section following this Introduction and review the typical development for your group of young children. This information can provide a framework for selecting appropriate books.

There are some general guidelines for selecting books. First, children enjoy books that relate to their experiences. They also enjoy action. The words written in the book should be simple, descriptive, and within the child's understanding. The pictures should be large, colorful, and closely represent the actions.

A book that is good for one group of children may be inappropriate for another. You must know the child or group of children for whom the story is being selected. Consider their interests, attention span, and developmental level.

Developmental considerations are important. Two-year-olds enjoy stories about the things they do, know, and enjoy. Commonplace adventure is a preference for three-year-olds. They like to listen to things that could happen to them, including stories about community helpers. Four-year-old children are not as self-centered. These children do not have to be part of every situation that they hear about. Many are ready for short and simple fantasy stories. Five-year-olds like stories that add to their knowledge, that is, books that contain new information.

Curriculum Planning Guide

We hope you find this book to be a valuable guide in planning curriculum. The ideas should help you build curriculum based upon the children's natural interests. The book should also give you ideas so that your program will provide a wide variety of choices for children.

In planning a developmentally valid curriculum, consult the Index by Subject. It has been prepared to allow you easy selection from all the themes. So pick and choose and make it your own! The Index is arranged by subject as follows:

—Art
—Cooking
—Dramatic Play
—Features (by Theme)
—Field Trips/Resource People
—Fingerplays
—Group Time
—Large Muscle
—Math
—Rain Day
—Science
—Sensory
—Songs

Other Sources

Early childhood educators should refer to other Delmar publications when developing appropriate curriculum, including:

1. Oppenheim, Carol. *Science is Fun!*
2. Green, Moira. *474 Science Activities for Young Children.*
3. Herr, Judy and Libby, Yvonne. *Creative Resources of Art, Brushes, Buildings . . .*
4. Herr, Judy and Libby, Yvonne. *Creative Resources of Birds, Animals, Seasons, and Holidays.*
5. Green, Moira. *Themes With a Difference: 228 New Activities for Young Children.*
6. Green, Moira. Not! *The Same Old Activities for Early Childhood.*
7. Mayesky, Mary. *Creative Activities for Young Children* (5th ed.).
8. Pica, Rae. *Experiences in Movement with Music, Activities, and Theory.*
9. American Chemical Society and American Institute of Physics. *The Best of WonderScience.*
10. Wheeler, Ron. *Creative Resources for Elementary Classrooms and School-Age Programs.*
11. Bouza-Koster, Joan. *Growing Artists.*
12. Herr, Judy and Libby, Yvonne. *Creative Resources for the Early Childhood Classroom* (2nd ed.).

DEVELOPMENTAL BENCHMARKS

Ages	Fine Motor Skills	Gross Motor Skills
Two Year Olds	Turns pages in a book singly Imitates drawing a circle, vertical, and horizontal lines Fingers work together to scoop up small objects Constructs simple two- and three-piece puzzles Enjoys short, simple fingerplay games Strings large beads on shoelace Builds tower of up to eight blocks	Kicks large ball Jumps in place Runs without falling Throws ball without falling Walks up and down stairs alone Marches to music Tends to use legs and arms as pairs Uses whole arm usually to paint or color
Three Year Olds	Cuts paper Builds tower of nine small blocks Pastes using a finger Pours from a pitcher Copies a circle from a drawing Draws a straight line Uses fingers to pick up small objects Draws a person with three parts Strings beads and can arrange by color and shape Uses a knife to spread at meal or snack time	Catches ball with arms extended forward Throws ball underhand Completes forward somersault Walks up stairs with alternating feet Rides a tricycle skillfully Runs, walks, jumps, and gallops to music Throws ball without losing balance Hops on one foot
Four Year Olds	Buttons or unbuttons buttons Cuts on a line with scissors Completes a six- to eight-piece puzzle Copies a "t" Buckles a belt Zips separated fasteners Adds five parts to an incomplete man	Walks up and down stairs one foot per step Skips on one foot Rides a bicycle with training wheels
Five Year Olds	Uses a knife Copies most letters Traces objects Draws crude objects Colors within lines Copies square, triangle, and diamond shape Models objects from clay Laces shoes	Tries roller and ice skating Catches ball with hands Jumps from heights Jumps rope Walks on stilts Skips Climbs fences
Six Year Olds	Ties bows Hand preference established Reverses letters while printing Paints houses, trees, flowers, and clouds	Plays hopscotch Enjoys ball play Plays simple, organized games such as "hide-and-seek"

DEVELOPMENTAL BENCHMARKS

Ages	Emotional and Social Skills	Intellectual Skills
Two Year Olds	Takes toys away from others Plays near other children, but not cooperatively Unable to share toys Acts negatively at times Seeks teacher's attention Expresses fear of the dark Observes others to see how they do things	Talks mostly to himself Uses "me" instead of proper name Enjoys showing and naming objects Uses a two- to three-hundred word vocabulary Speaks in phrases or three-word sentences Answers yes/no questions Follows two-step commands Constructs negative sentences (no truck, no truck) Uses modifiers such as some, all, one Understands concepts big and little Uses such adjectives as red, old, and pretty
Three Year Olds	Plays in groups of two or three children Begins to take turns Sharing becomes evident with friends Enjoys independence by doing things for themselves, i.e., "Let me do it" or "I can do it." Yells "stop it" at times, as opposed to striking another child	Asks "how," "what," "when," and "why" questions Uses verb such as "could," "needs," "might," and "help" Uses adverbs such as "how about" and "maybe" Understands the pronouns you and they Understands "smaller" and "larger" Answers "how" questions appropriately Loves words such as "secret," "surprise," and "different" Uses words to define space such as "back," "up," "outside," "in front of," "in back of," "over," "next to"
Four Year Olds	Loves other children and having a "friend" Bases friendships on shared activities Seeks approval of friends Plays with small groups of children Delights in humorous stories Shows more interest in other children than adults Excludes children he does not like Loves to whisper and tell secrets	Experiences trouble telling the difference between reality and fantasy Exaggerates in practicing new words Loves silly language and to repeat new silly words Vocabulary of 1200 to 1500 words Begins to identify letters in his name Begins to appreciate bugs, trees, flowers, and birds Learns simple card games and dominoes Develops an awareness of "bad" and "good"
Five Year Olds	Prefers playing in small groups Prefers friends of same sex and age Protects younger children Plays well with older siblings Washes hands before meals Respects other people's property Becomes competitive Develops sense of fairness Verbally expresses anger	Names the days of the week Writes numbers from one to ten Retells main details of stories Recognizes the cause and effect of actions Uses a vocabulary of 2000 or more words Tells original stories Follows three-step command Recognizes square and rectangle shape Recognizes numerals 1-5
Six Year Olds	Prefers friends of the same sex Engages in cooperative play involving role assignments Enjoys being praised and complimented Enjoys "show and tell" time May be argumentative Competitive and wants to win	Identifies penny, nickel, and dime Counts ten objects Completes a 15-piece puzzle Acts out stories Plays Chinese checkers and dominoes Recognizes letters and words in books Identifies right from left hand Prints numbers from 1-20 Repeats an 8-10 word sentence Counts numbers to 30

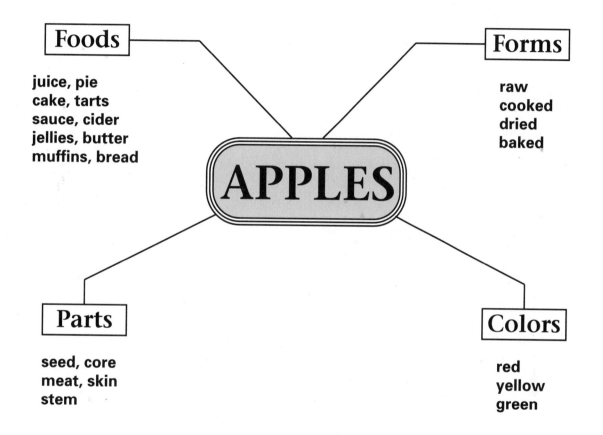

Foods

juice, pie
cake, tarts
sauce, cider
jellies, butter
muffins, bread

Forms

raw
cooked
dried
baked

APPLES

Parts

seed, core
meat, skin
stem

Colors

red
yellow
green

Theme Goals:

Through participating in the experiences provided by this theme, the children may learn:

1. Parts of an apple.

2. Preparation of apples for eating.

3. Apple tastes.

4. Textures, sizes, and colors of apples.

5. The origin of an apple.

Concepts for the Children to Learn:

1. An apple is a fruit.

2. An apple has five parts: seed, core, meat, skin, and stem.

3. Apples grow on trees.

4. A group of apple trees is an orchard.

5. Bread, butter, cakes, pies, pudding, applesauce, dumplings, butter, and jelly can be prepared from apples.

6. Some apples are sweet; others are sour.

7. Apples can be green, yellow, or red.

8. Apples can be large or small.

9. Apples can be hard or soft.

10. Seeds from an apple can grow into a tree.

Vocabulary:

1. **apple**—a fruit that is grown on a tree.

2. **texture**—how something feels.

3. **core**—the part of the apple that contains seeds.

4. **apple blossom**—a flower on the apple tree.

5. **apple butter**—a spread for bread made from apples.

Bulletin Board

The purpose of this bulletin board is to develop the mathematical skill of sets, as well as to identify written numerals. Construct red apples. The number will depend upon the developmental level of the children. Laminate the apples. Collect containers for baskets, such as large cottage cheese or pint berry containers. Cover the containers with paper if necessary. Affix numerals on baskets, beginning with the numeral 1. Staple the baskets to the bulletin board. The object is for the children to place the appropriate number of apples in each basket.

Parent Letter

Dear Parents,

Is it true that "an apple a day keeps the doctor away?" I'm not sure, but the children will make many discoveries as we begin a new unit on apples at school. Through active exploration and interaction, they will become more aware of the different flavors of apples, colors of apples, and ways apples can be prepared and eaten.

At School

Some classroom activities for this unit include:
- preparing applesauce for Thursday's snack.
- drying apples in the sun.
- creating apple-shaped sponge prints in the art area.
- visiting the apple orchard! Arrangements have been made for a tour of the apple orchard on Wednesday morning. We will be leaving the center at 10:00 a.m. Feel free to join us.

At Home

Apples are a tasty and nutritious food—and most children enjoy eating them. Try a variety of apples for meals or snacks. You might also enjoy preparing caramel apples with your child. A recipe is as follows:

1 pound of vanilla caramels
2 tablespoons of water
dash of salt
6 crisp apples
6 wooden skewers or popsicle sticks

Melt the caramels with water in a microwave oven or double boiler, stirring frequently until smooth. Stir in the salt and stick a wooden skewer or popsicle stick in each apple. Dip the apple into the syrup, turning until the surface of the apple is completely covered.

Cooking is a great way to learn by experience because it involves the whole child—physically, emotionally, socially, and intellectually. It also builds vocabulary and involves amounts, measuring, and fractions, which are mathematical concepts. When a recipe is used, your child will also learn to follow a sequence. Enjoy cooking with your child.

Enjoy an apple with your child today!

Music:

1. **"If I Had an Apple"**
   (Sing to the tune of "If I Had a Hammer")

   If I had an apple
   I'd eat it in the morning,
   I'd eat it in the evening,
   All over this land.
   I'd eat it for breakfast,
   I'd eat it for supper,
   I'd eat it with all my friends and sisters and brothers
   All, all over this land.

   Source: Chenfield, Mimi Brodsky. *Creative Activities for Young Children.*

2. **"Little Apples"**
   (Sing to the tune of "Ten Little Indians")

   One little, two little, three little apples,
   Four little, five little, six little apples,
   Seven little, eight little, nine little apples,
   All fell to the ground.

   A variation for older children would be to give each child a number card (with a numeral from 1 through 9). When that number is sung, that child stands up. At the end of the fingerplay all the children fall down.

3. **"Apples Off My Tree"**
   (Sing to the tune of "Skip to My Lou")

   Pick some apples off my tree,
   Pick some apples off my tree,
   Pick some apples off my tree,
   Pick them all for you and me.

4. **"My Apple Tree"**
   (Sing to the tune of "The Muffin Man")

   Did you see my apple tree,
   Did you see my apple tree,
   Did you see my apple tree,
   Full of apples red?

Fingerplays:

APPLE TREE

Way up high in the apple tree
   (stretch arm up high)
Two little apples smiled at me.
   (hold up 2 fingers)
I shook that tree as hard as I could
   (make shaking motion)
Down came the apples.
   (make downward motions)
Mmmm—they were good.
   (smile and rub stomach)

PICKING APPLES

Here's a little apple tree.
   (left arm up, fingers spread)
I look up and I can see
   (look at fingers)
Big red apples, ripe and sweet,
   (cup hands to hold apple)
Big red apples, good to eat!
   (raise hands to mouth)
Shake the little apple tree.
   (shake tree with hands)
See the apples fall on me.
   (raise cupped hands and let fall)
Here's a basket, big and round.
   (make circle with arms)
Pick the apples from the ground.
   (pick and put in basket)
Here's an apple I can see.
   (look up to the tree)
I'll reach up. It's ripe and sweet.
   (reach up to upper hand)
That's the apple I will eat!
   (hands to mouth)

AN APPLE

An apple is what I'd like to be.
My shape would be round.
   (fingers in circular shape)
My color would be green.
   (point to something green)
Children could eat me each and every day.
I'm good in tarts and pies and cakes.
   (make these food shapes)
An apple is good to eat or to bake.
   (make stirring motion)

Help children discover all the wonderful foods prepared from apples.

THE APPLE

Within its polished universe
The apple holds a star.
(draw design of star with index finger)
A secret constellation
To scatter near and far.
(point near and far)
Let a knife discover
Where the five points hide.
Split the shiny ruby
And find the star inside.

After introducing the fingerplay the teacher can cut an apple crosswise to find a star.

APPLE TREE

This is the tree
With leaves so green.
(make leaves with fingers outstretched)

Here are the apples
That hang in between.
(make fist)
When the wind blows
(blow)
The apples will fall.
(falling motion with hand)
Here is the basket to gather them all.
(use arms to form basket)

Sensory:

1. Cut different varieties of apples for a tasting party. This activity can easily be extended. On another day provide the children applesauce, apple pie, apple juice, or apple cider to taste during snack or lunch.
2. Place several different kinds of seeds on the sensory table. In addition, to create interest provide scoops, bowls, and bottles to fill.

Math:

1. Cut apple shapes of various sizes from construction paper. Let the children sequence the shapes from smallest to largest.
2. Place a scale and various-sized apples on the math table. The children can experiment by weighing the apples.

Science:

1. **Solar Baked Apple Slices**

   Materials: 4 styrofoam cups
   black paper
   scissors
   masking tape
   apple
   knife
   plastic wrap
   rubber bands
   white paper
   foil
   newspaper

   Line 2 cups with black paper. Place 2 equal-sized slices of apple inside each cup. Cover with plastic wrap held by rubber band. With paper and tape make a cone. Place one apple cup into it. Cover the inside of another paper cone with aluminum foil and place second apple cup into it. Place both in a sunny window facing the sun on crumpled newspaper. Which one cooks faster? The apple baked in the aluminum foil.

Source: Sisson, Edith A. *Nature With Children of All Ages.*

2. **Dried Apples**

Peel, core, and cut apples into slices or rings about 1/8 inch thick. Prepare a salt water solution by mixing a tablespoon of salt in a gallon of water. Place the apples in this solution for several minutes. Remove from the solution. Place the apples in 180-degree oven for 3 to 4 hours or until dry. Turn the apples occasionally.

3. **Oxidation of an Apple**

Cut and core an apple into sections. Dip half the apple into lemon juice and place it on a plate. Place the remaining sections of apple on another plate. What happens to each plate of apples? Discuss the effects of the lemon juice coating which keeps oxygen from the apples. As a result, they do not discolor as rapidly.

4. **Explore an Apple**

Discuss the color, size, and shape of an apple. Then discuss the parts of an apple. Include the skin, stem, core, meat, etc. Feel the apple. Then cut the apple in half. Observe the core and seeds. An apple is a fruit because it contains seeds.

Dramatic Play:

Set Up an Apple Stand

Prepare an apple stand by providing the children with bags, plastic apples, cash register, money, stand, and bushels. Encourage buying, selling, and packaging.

Arts and Crafts:

1. **Apple Printing**

Cut apple shapes from sponges. Have available individual shallow pans of red, yellow, and green tempera paint. Provide paper. The apple can be used as a painting tool. To illustrate, the children can place an apple half in the paint. After removing the excess paint, the apple can be placed on paper to create a print.

2. **Seed Pictures**

Collect: apple seeds along with other seeds
paper
colors
glue

Each child who chooses to participate should be provided a small number of seeds. As they are distributed, discuss the seeds' similarities and differences. Provide uninterrupted time for the children to glue seeds onto paper and create pictures.

3. **Shakers**

Collect: appleseeds
paper plates (2 per child)
glue or stapler
color crayons or felt-tip markers

The children can decorate the paper plates with color crayons or felt-tip markers. After this, the seeds can be placed between the two plates. To create the shakers, staple or glue the two plates together by securing the outer edges of the plates. The children can use the shakers as a means of self expression during music or self-directed play.

Field Trips:

1. **Visit an Apple Orchard**

Observe the workers picking, sorting, and/or selling the apples. Call attention to the colors and types of apples.

2. Visit a Grocery Store

Observe all the forms of apples sold in a grocery store. Also, in the produce department, observe the different colors and sizes of apples. To show children differences in weight, take a large apple and place on a scale. Note the weight. Then take a small apple and repeat the process.

Group Time (games, language):

1. What Is It?

Collect a variety of fruits such as an apple, banana, and orange. Begin by placing one fruit in a bag. Choose a child to touch the fruit, describe it, and name it. Repeat with each fruit, discussing the characteristics. During the activity each child should have an opportunity to participate.

2. Transition Activity

The children should stand in a circle. As a record is played, the children pass an apple. When the record stops, the child holding the apple can get up to get a snack, put on outdoor clothes, clean up, etc. Continue until all children have a turn. For older children, more than one apple may be successfully passed at a time.

Cooking:

1. Caramel Apple Slices

Prepare the following recipe, which should serve 12 to 14 children.

1 pound caramels
2 tablespoons water
dash of salt
6 crisp apples

Melt caramels with water in the microwave oven or double boiler, stirring frequently until melted. Stir in the salt. Pour the melted caramel over the sliced apples and cool before serving.

2. Applesauce

30 large apples
2 1/2 cups water
1 1/2 cups sugar
1 tablespoon red hots

1. Clean apples by peeling, coring, and cutting into small pieces.
2. Place the apples in a large kettle containing water.
3. Simmer the apples on low heat, stirring occasionally until soft.
4. Add the remaining ingredients.
5. Stir and simmer a few minutes.
6. Cool prior to eating.

3. Persian Apple Dessert

3 medium apples, cut up
2 to 3 tablespoons sugar
2 tablespoons lemon juice
dash of salt

Place half the apples and the remaining ingredients in a blender. Cover and blend until coarsely chopped, about 20 to 30 seconds. Add remaining apples and repeat. Makes 3 servings.

4. Charoses

6 medium apples
1/2 cup raisins
1/2 teaspoon cinnamon
1/2 cup chopped nuts
1/4 cup white grape juice

Chop the peeled or unpeeled apples. Add the remaining ingredients. Mix well and serve.

5. Fruit Leather

2 cups applesauce
vegetable shortening or oil

Preheat oven to 400 degrees. Pour applesauce onto greased shallow pan. Spread to 1/8 inch in thickness. Place pan in oven and lower temperature to 180 degrees. Cook for approximately 3 hours until the leather can be peeled from the pan. Cut with scissors to serve.

6. Dried Apples

5 or 6 apples
2 tablespoons salt
water

Peel, core, and cut apples into slices or rings 1/8 inch thick. Place apple slices in salt-water solution (2 tablespoons per 1 gallon water) for several minutes. Remove from the water. Place in 180-degree oven for 3 to 4 hours until dry. Turn apples occasionally.

Books:

The following books can be used to complement this theme:

1. Rockwell, Anne. (1989). *Apples and Pumpkins*. New York: Macmillan.
2. Gibbons, Gail. (1984). *The Seasons of Arnold's Appletree*. San Diego, CA: Harcourt Brace Jovanovich.
3. *Apple Tree! Apple Tree! Big Book*. (1990). Emeryville, CA: Children's Press.
4. Genet, Barbara. (1985). *To-Poo-Ach Means Apple*. ARE Publishers.
5. *Who Took Apple Frapple's Cookbook?* (1992). Mentor, OH: Glue Books.
6. Maestro, Betsy. (1992). *How Do Apples Grow?* New York: Harper Collins.

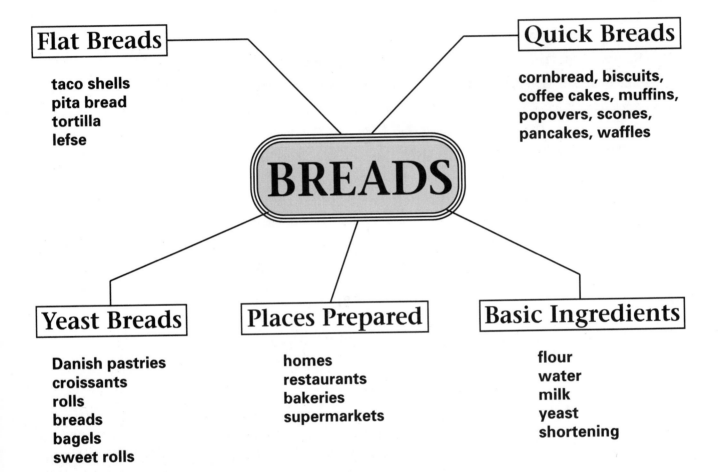

Flat Breads

taco shells
pita bread
tortilla
lefse

Quick Breads

cornbread, biscuits,
coffee cakes, muffins,
popovers, scones,
pancakes, waffles

BREADS

Yeast Breads

Danish pastries
croissants
rolls
breads
bagels
sweet rolls

Places Prepared

homes
restaurants
bakeries
supermarkets

Basic Ingredients

flour
water
milk
yeast
shortening

Theme Goals:

Through participating in the experiences provided by this theme, the children may learn:

1. The basic ingredients of bread.

2. Places bread is prepared.

3. Types of yeast bread.

4. Types of flat bread.

5. Types of quick bread.

Concepts for the Children to Learn:

1. There are many kinds of breads.

2. Breads are important for good health.

3. Bread is the most widely eaten food.

4. The basic ingredients used in preparing bread are flour, water and/or milk, and shortening.

5. Bread can be prepared in homes, bakeries, supermarkets, and restaurants.

6. Breads can be large or small in size.

7. Breads can have different flavors.

8. Some breads contain a fruit filling and are called sweet rolls.

9. Breads can be shaped into different forms: round, twisted, and oblong.

10. Breads can be hard or soft.

11. Breads can be part of a meal or snack.

Vocabulary:

1. **bread**—a food prepared by mixing flour or grain meal with water or milk and shortening.

2. **crust**—the outside part of the bread.

3. **leaven**—a food that makes the bread dough rise.

4. **flour**—wheat that has been ground to a soft powder.

Bulletin Board

The purpose of this bulletin board is to promote visual discrimination skills and call attention to various types of baked goods. Create this bulletin board by drawing baked goods on a piece of tagboard as illustrated. Pictures from magazines could also be used. If drawn, color the bakery items with markers, cut out, and laminate. Trace these pieces onto black construction paper. Count out the pieces and attach to the bulletin board. Use map tacks or adhesive magnet pieces for children to match the corresponding baked good to its shadow.

Parent Letter

Dear Parents,

Did you know that bread is the most widely eaten food? It is often called the "staff of life" and it provides a large share of people's energy and protein. Our next curriculum will focus on a theme related to breads. Activities will help your child learn the different types of bread and the ingredients of bread, including the purpose of yeast. Your child will also participate in making bread. Special breads are also used in different cultural ceremonies.

At School

Some of the curriculum activities related to the theme will include:

- Tasting may kinds of breads.
- Sorting and then eating pretzels of various sizes and shapes.
- Baking bread on Thursday and observing the action of yeast.
- Making and selling baked goods in the Bakery Shop located in the dramatic play area.

At Home

We encourage you to participate in our celebration of bread. The next time you and your child are in the grocery store, find the bakery or bread department. Point out the different types and sizes of breads. Ask questions to help your child recognize similarities and differences.

Bake breads with your child and create warm family memories. Here is a simple recipe that you may want to try:

Zucchini Bread

1 1/2 cups all-purpose flour	1/4 cup cooking oil
3/4 cup sugar	1/4 teaspoon nutmeg
1 teaspoon ground cinnamon	1 beaten egg
1/2 teaspoon baking soda	1/4 teaspoon finely shredded lemon peel
1/4 teaspoon salt	1 cup shredded zucchini
1/4 teaspoon baking powder	1/2 cup chopped walnuts

Grease an 8x4x2-inch loaf pan. In a medium bowl mix together flour, sugar, cinnamon, baking powder, and nutmeg. Make well in the center of the dry mixture and add the zucchini. Stir only until mixture is folded in. Add the chopped walnuts.

Pour batter into the prepared loaf pan. Bake in a preheated oven set at 350 degrees for 55 to 60 minutes. Remove from the oven and cool on a wire rack for 10–12 minutes. Remove the bread from the pan and continue cooling on the wire rack. Wrap when cooled and let sit overnight before slicing.

A variation of this recipe would be to substitute shredded apples for the zucchini.

Enjoy a slice of bread with your child today!

It's tasty trying different kinds of bread and pastries.

Music:

1. **"If I had a Bagel"**
(Sing to the tune "If I Had a Hammer")

If I had a bagel.
I'd eat it in the morning,
I'd eat it in the evening,
All over this land.
I'd eat it for breakfast,
I'd eat it for supper,
I'd eat it with all my friends and sisters
and brothers,
All, all over this land.

2. **"Little Donuts"**
(Sing to the tune of "Ten Little Indians")

One little, two little, three little donuts
Four little, five little, six little donuts
Seven little, eight little, nine little donuts
Ten donuts in the bakery shop.

3. **"Let's Pretend"**
(Sing to the tune of "Here We Are Together")

Let's pretend that we are bakers,
Are bakers, are bakers
Let's pretend that we are bakers,
As busy as can be.
We'll knead all the dough out
And bake loaves of bread.
Let's pretend that we are bakers
As busy as can be.

Fingerplay:

FIVE LITTLE DONUTS

Down around the corner, at the bakery shop
There were five little donuts with sugar on top.
 (hold up five fingers)
Along came _____ (child's name), all alone.
And she/he took the biggest one home.

Continue the verses until all the donuts are
gone.

Science:

1. **Bread Grains**

On the science table set out containers of
grains used to make bread for the children to
examine. Examples include wheat, corn, oats,
and rye. Provide magnifying glasses for
children to explore the grains.

2. **Weighing Bread Grains**

The property of mass can be explored by providing a balance scale and bread grains at the science table. Scoops and spoons could be available to assist the children.

3. **Baking Bread**

The process of bread baking is definitely a science activity. The children can observe changes in substances and make predictions about the final outcome. Choose a bread recipe listed under the cooking section of this theme. Prepare a recipe chart for classroom use. Stress cooking safety with the children.

Dramatic Play:

1. **Bakery**

Prepare the housekeeping area to resemble a bakery where the children can pretend to make breads and bake goods to sell to their classmates as customers. Provide the following items: aprons, baker's hats, bowls, mixing spoons, pans, rolling pins, muffin tins, measuring cups, egg cartons, empty bread/roll mix boxes, oven mitts or hot pads, a cash register, and poster/pictures depicting baked goods.

2. **Restaurant**

Prepare the housekeeping area as a restaurant. Provide props such as a table cloth, dishes, cooking utensils, and a cash register with play money. Create menus by cutting pictures from magazines and gluing onto construction paper. Include pictures of different baked goods.

Arts and Crafts:

1. **Bread Collage**

Provide magazines for the children to find and cut out pictures of different types of breads. These pictures can be glued or pasted to a piece of construction paper or a paper plate, creating a bread collage.

2. **Play Dough**

The children can assist in preparing play dough. If the mixture is left uncolored, it will resemble bread dough and have a similar consistency. Place three cups of flour and one cup of salt in a mixing bowl. Add 3/4 cup of water and stir. Keep adding small amounts of water and mix until the dough is workable, but not sticky.

3. **Muffin Tin Paint Trays**

Fill muffin tins with various colors of paint in the art area for the children to use. Pastry brushes could be used as paint applicators.

4. **Biscuit Cutter Prints**

Place biscuit cutters and a shallow pan of paint out at the art table. The children can dip the biscuit cutter into the paint. After this, the biscuit cutter can be placed on a piece of construction paper. The children can repeat the process as desired.

5. **Bread Sponge Painting**

Cut sponges into different shapes and types of bread. Place the sponges and shallow trays of tempera paint on the art table. The children can dip a sponge into the paint and then press it onto a piece of paper to create a bread-shaped print.

Sensory:

1. Different types of grains can be placed in the sensory table. Examples include corn, rice, wheat, barley, and oats. Provide pails, scoops, measuring cups, flour sifters, and spoons to encourage active exploration.
2. Place play dough in the sensory table with rolling pins, measuring cups, muffin tins, and plastic knives.
3. Cooking utensils used for preparing baked goods can be placed in the sensory table with soapy water and dish cloths. The children can "wash" the items.

Large Muscle:

1. **Tricycles**

   During outdoor play, encourage children to use the tricycles for making bakery deliveries.

2. **Bread Trail**

   Set up a bread trail in the classroom. Tape pictures of the bread creating a trail on the floor. Have the children follow the trail by walking or hopping.

Field Trips:

1. **Bakery**

   Arrange a visit to a local bakery. Observe the process of bread and baked goods production. Discuss a baker's job and uniform.

2. **Farm**

   Take a trip to a farm where grains are grown. Notice the equipment and machinery used to plant and harvest the crops.

3. **Grocery Store**

   Tour a grocery store and find the bakery department. The children can look at the many types of breads and ways they are packaged.

Math:

1. **Favorite Bread Graph**

   After tasting various types of breads, the children can assist in making a class graph of their favorite types of breads. Across the top of a piece of tagboard, print the caption "Our Favorite Breads." Draw or paste pictures of different types or flavors of breads along the left-hand side of the tagboard.

   On the chart, place each child's name or picture next to the picture of his/her favorite bread. The results of the graph can be shared with the children using math vocabulary words such as most, more, fewer, least, etc. Display the graph for future reference.

2. **Muffin Tin Math**

   Muffin tins can be used for counting and sorting activities based upon the children's developmental level. For example, numerals can be printed in each cup, and the children can place the corresponding set of corn or toy pieces in each cup. Likewise, colored circles can be cut out of construction paper and glued to the bottom of the muffin cups. The children then can place objects of matching colors in the corresponding muffin cups.

3. **Pretzel Sort and Count**

   Provide each child with a cup containing various sizes and shapes of pretzels. Encourage the children to empty the cup onto a clean napkin or plate and sort the pretzels by size or shape. If appropriate, the children can count how many pretzels they have of each shape. Upon completion of the activity, the pretzels can be eaten by the children.

4. **Breadstick Seriation**

   Provide breadsticks or pictures of breadsticks of varying lengths. The children can place the breadsticks in order from shortest to longest.

Social Studies:

1. **Baker**

   The occupation of baker can be examined through books and discussion.

2. **Sharing Breads**

   Bake breads or muffins to give to a home for the elderly, the homeless, or some other organization. If possible, take a walk and have the children deliver them.

3. **Visitor**

   Invite people from various cultural backgrounds to bake or share breads originating from their native countries. As a follow-up activity, assist the children in writing thank-you notes.

Group Time (games, language):

1. **Bread-Tasting Party**

   Bake or purchase various types and flavors of breads. Cut the bread into small pieces and place these samples on paper plates for the children to taste. Discuss the types of breads, textures, flavors, and scents.

2. **Yeast Experiment**

   To demonstrate the effects of yeast, try this experiment. Pour one package of dry yeast, 1/2 cup of sugar, and one cup of warm water into an empty soda bottle. Cover the bottle opening with a balloon and watch it expand.

3. **The Little Red Hen**

   Read the story of *The Little Red Hen* by Paul Galdone. After reading the story several times so that the children are familiar with the content, it can be acted out. Simple props can be provided to assist the children in creative dramatics and recreating the story.

4. **Bread Basket Upset**

   This game is played in a circle formation on chairs or carpet squares. One child is asked to sit in the middle of the circle as the baker. Hand a picture of various breads—breads, rolls, muffins, etc.—to each of the other children. To play the game, the baker calls out the name of a bread. The children holding that particular bread exchange places. The game continues. When the baker calls out, "Bread Basket Upset," all of the children must exchange places, including the baker. The child who is unable to find a place is the new baker.

Cooking:

1. **Bag Bread**

   Collect the following ingredients:

   3 cups of bread flour
   2 packages of fast-rising yeast
   1/4 cup sugar

   1 1/2 teaspoon salt
   1 1/2 cup warm water (125 to 130 degrees)
   4 teaspoons vegetable oil

   In a gallon-sized heavy plastic zip-lock freezer bag place 1 1/2 cup flour, dry yeast, and salt. Close. Let the children mix the ingredients by shaking and working the bag with their fingers to blend the ingredients.

   Add the oil and warm water to the ingredients in the bag. Reseal the bag and demonstrate to the children how to mix the ingredients. Gradually add the remaining flour until the mixture forms a stiff ball.

   Grease your hands with a solid vegetable oil. Remove the dough from the bag and place on a lightly floured surface. Knead about five minutes. Small air pockets that appear as bubbles will form under the surface of the dough when it has been sufficiently kneaded. When they appear, let the children observe them.

   Let the dough rest for 5–10 minutes. Grease two bread pans. Divide the dough in half. Shape into two loaves. Place each loaf in a greased bread pan. Cover with a kitchen towel. Let rise for an hour. Bake at 375 degrees for 25–30 minutes.

2. **Pretzels**

   Collect the following ingredients:

   1 teaspoon salt
   2 1/2 teaspoons sugar
   1 package of fast-rising yeast
   1 cup warm water (125 to 130 degrees).
   1 tablespoon vegetable oil
   1 egg yolk, beaten with 1 tablespoon water
   3–3 1/2 cups flour

   Combine 1 1/2 cups of flour, the dry yeast, sugar, and salt in a large bowl. Add the warm water and vegetable oil and mix at low speed with an electric mixer for three minutes. Add an additional 1/2 cup flour and beat at high speed for 2–3 minutes. WHILE USING THE ELECTRIC MIXER THIS ACTIVITY NEEDS TO BE CAREFULLY SUPERVISED. Stir in the remaining flour to form a soft dough.

   Lightly flour a surface. Place the soft dough on the floured surface and knead for approximately 10 minutes. Grease a bowl with vegetable oil and place the dough in to rise. Cover with a dish towel for 30-45 minutes.

Punch the air out of the dough and divide into 20 equal pieces. Demonstrate to the children how to roll a piece into a rope 12–14 inches long. Form the rope into a pretzel. Place on a greased baking sheet. Cover again and let rise in a warm place for about 25 minutes.

Brush each of the pretzels with the egg yolk mixture. Preheat the oven to 375 degrees. Bake for 15 minutes and remove from pan. Place on a wire rack to cool.

3. Chappatis

This recipe, which comes from India, serves 6; consequently, it will need to be adjusted to accommodate the number of children who need to be served.

1 1/2 cups of whole wheat flour
1/2 teaspoon salt
2/3 cup warm water
a small amount of cooking oil

Mix the flour and salt together in a bowl. Stir in water a small amount at a time until the mixture forms a ball.

On a floured surface, knead dough for 5–10 minutes, until it is a smooth, sticky ball. Let rise in a covered bowl for 30 minutes.

Cut the dough into six pieces. Roll each piece out into a circle that is about eight inches in diameter.

Lightly oil a frying pan with oil and heat until it smokes. THIS PORTION OF THE ACTIVITY NEEDS TO BE CAREFULLY SUPERVISED TO PROMOTE A SAFE ENVIRONMENT. Cook each circle of dough until it is brown and puffy on both sides. The chappatis is more flavorful when eaten warm.

4. Cheesy Puff Bread

3 3/4 cups of bread flour
1 package rapid-rise dry yeast
1 teaspoon salt
1/2 cup milk
2 tablespoons margarine
2 eggs
1 cup grated cheddar cheese
1/2 cup warm water
3 tablespoons sugar

Combine the dry yeast, sugar, salt, and 1 1/2 cups of flour in a large mixing bowl. Heat the milk, water, and margarine on the stove or in the microwave oven until warm to the touch. Add the dry ingredients. Then beat at low speed with an electric mixer. Add 1/2 cup of flour and the eggs. Beat at high speed for 2–3 minutes. Stir in the cheese and enough flour to make a soft dough.

On a lightly floured surface, knead the dough until it is elastic and smooth. Typically this will take 6–10 minutes. Place the dough in a greased bowl and let rise for 15–30 minutes.

Grease the entire inner surface of two l-lb. coffee cans. Divide the dough into two equal pieces. Place each piece in a can. Cover the top of the can with a piece of aluminum foil. Let the dough rise for 35 minutes.

Bake for 30 minutes in a 375-degree oven. Remove from cans and cool on a wire rack.

Multimedia:

The following resources can be found in educational catalogs:

1. Raffi. "Biscuits in the Ocean" on *Baby Beluga* [record].

2. Greg & Steve. "Muffin Man" on *We All Live Together—Volume Z* [record].

3. Sharon, Lois, & Bram. *Elephant Show Record* [record].

4. Sharon, Lois, & Bram. "Five Brown Buns" on *Books and Stories* [record].

Books:

The following books can be used to complement this theme:

1. Morris, Ann. (1989). *Bread, Bread, Bread*. New York: Lothrop.

2. Robbins, Ken. (1992). *Make Me a Peanut Butter Sandwich and a Glass of Milk*. New York: Scholastic, Inc.

3. Mancure, Jane. (1985). *What Was It Before It Was Bread?* Mankato, MN: Child's World, Inc.

4. Ziegler, Sandra. (1987). *A Visit to the Bakery*. Chicago: Children's Press.

5. Spohn, Kate. (1990). *Ruth's Bake Shop*. New York: Orchard Books.

6. dePaola, Tomie. (1989). *Tony's Bread*. New York: Putnam Publishing.

7. Galdone, Paul. (1975). *The Little Red Hen*. Boston: Houghton Mifflin Co.

8. Asch, Frank. (1992). *Bread and Honey*. New York: Putnam Publishing.

9. Lord, John V., & Burroway. (1990). *Giant Jam Sandwich*. Boston: Houghton Mifflin Co.

10. Lillegard, Dee. (1986). *I Can Be A Baker*. Chicago: Children's Press.

11. Kingston, Arlene. (1988). *The Bagels Are Coming*. West Bloomfield, MI.: Child Time Publishers.

12. McLean, Bill. (1990). *The Best Peanut Butter Sandwich in the Whole World*. Buffalo, NY: Firefly Books.

13. Dragonwagon, Crescent. (1989). *This Is the Bread I Baked for Ned*. New York: Macmillan.

THEME 3

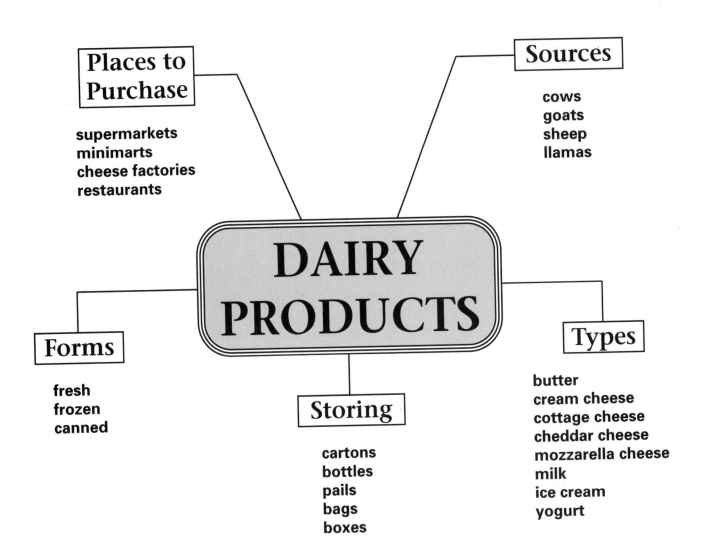

Places to Purchase

supermarkets
minimarts
cheese factories
restaurants

Sources

cows
goats
sheep
llamas

DAIRY PRODUCTS

Forms

fresh
frozen
canned

Storing

cartons
bottles
pails
bags
boxes

Types

butter
cream cheese
cottage cheese
cheddar cheese
mozzarella cheese
milk
ice cream
yogurt

Theme Goals:

Through participating in the experiences provided by this theme, the children may learn:

1. Sources of dairy products.

2. Types of dairy products.

3. Forms of dairy products.

4. Places dairy products can be purchased.

5. Containers used to hold dairy products.

Concepts for the Children to Learn:

1. Cows, goats, sheep, and llamas provide milk.

2. Milk can be used to make butter, cheese, ice cream, and yogurt.

3. There are many kinds of cheese such as cottage cheese, cream cheese, cheddar cheese, mozzarella, and colby.

4. Dairy products can be purchased fresh, frozen, canned, or processed.

5. We can buy dairy products at supermarkets, minimarts, cheese factories, and restaurants.

6. Cartons, bottles, pails, bags, and boxes are used to store dairy products.

7. Dairy products are good food choices.

Vocabulary:

1. **dairy product**—a product made from milk.

2. **can**—to prepare food for future use.

3. **frozen**—food that is kept cold.

4. **cheese factory**—a place where cheese is made or sold.

5. **carton**—a box or container to hold food or other objects.

6. **cream**—the yellowish part of milk.

7. **yogurt**—a milk product that can be flavored with fruit.

8. **minimart**—a very small store.

Bulletin Board

The purpose of this bulletin board is to help children become aware of ice cream as a dairy product, as well as recognize the printed word. This is designed as a check-in bulletin board. Each child is provided a bulletin board piece with his name on it. When the children arrive each day at school, they place their name on the bulletin board.

To create the bulletin board, cut an ice cream cone out of tagboard or construction paper for each child in the class. Color or decorate each cone as desired. Print the child's name on the ice cream cone. Laminate the pieces or cover with clear contact paper. Use push pins or adhesive magnet pieces to attach the ice cream cones to the bulletin board.

Parent Letter

Dear Parent:

Did you know that, on average, each person in the United States consumes about 550 pounds of dairy products each year? Dairy products provide us with one of our main sources of protein. We will study dairy products in our classroom. The children will learn sources of dairy products, types of dairy products, forms of dairy products, places dairy products can be purchased, and containers used to hold dairy products.

At School

Some of the learning activities the children will participate in include:

- Preparing milkshakes, homemade vanilla pudding, and strawberry yogurt in the cooking area.
- Creating a dairy collage, yogurt print cups, and ice cream cone sponge paints in the art area.
- Hearing stories related to the story theme.
- Visiting the dairy department of a grocery store.

At Home

At home you can reinforce the dairy product concepts by:

- Encouraging your child to prepare instant pudding with you for snack or a desert.
- At mealtimes, have your child identify the foods being served that are dairy products.
- Browse through newspaper ads or magazines and have your child identify dairy products.
- Take your child grocery shopping and have him show you where the dairy section of the store is located.

Enjoy your child!

Milk is a dairy product.

Music:

1. **"The Farmer in the Dell"**

   The farmer in the dell,
   The farmer in the dell,
   Hi-ho, the dairy-o
   The farmer in the dell.

   Continue with additional verses:

   The farmer takes the wife/husband
   The wife/husband takes the nurse.
   The nurse takes the dog.
   The dog takes the cat.
   The cat takes the rat.
   The rat takes the cheese.

   The final verse:

   The cheese stands alone.
   The cheese stands alone.
   Hi-ho, the dairy-o,
   The cheese stands alone.

2. **"Old McDonald Had a Farm"** (traditional)

3. **"We Like Ice Cream"**
   (Sing to the tune of "Are You Sleeping?")

   We like ice cream, we like ice cream.
   Yes, we do! Yes, we do!
   Vanilla and strawberry,
   Chocolate and mint.
   Yum, yum, yum.
   Yum, yum, yum!

4. **"Drink Your Milk"**
   (Sing to the tune of "My Darling Clementine")

   Drink your milk.
   Drink your milk.
   Drink your milk everyday.
   It is good for your teeth and bones.
   Drink your milk everyday.

5. **"Cows"**
   (Sing to the tune of "Mulberry Bush")

   This is the way we feed the cows,
   Feed the cows, feed the cows.
   This is the way we feed the cows,
   On the dairy farm each day.

   This is the way we milk the cows,
   Milk the cows, milk the cows.
   This is the way we milk the cows,
   On the dairy farm each day.

Fingerplays:

ICE CREAM

I'm licking my ice cream.
I'm licking it fast.
It's dripping down my arm.
It's disappearing fast.

LITTLE MISS MUFFET

Little Miss Muffet
Sat on a tuffet
Eating her curds and whey.
Along came a spider
And sat down beside her
And frightened Miss Muffet away!

THIS LITTLE COW

This little cow eats grass.
  (hold up fingers of one hand, bend down
  one finger)
This little cow eats hay.
  (bend down another finger)
This little cow drinks water.
  (bend down another finger)
And this little cow does nothing.
  (bend down another finger)
But lie and sleep all day.

Science:

1. Make Butter

Fill baby food jars half-full with whipping cream and replace lids. The children can take turns shaking the jars until the cream separates. (The mixture will first look like whipping cream, then like overwhipped cream, and finally it will be obvious that separation has occurred.) Pour off the remaining liquid. Rinse the butter in cold water several times and drain. Add salt to taste. Let the children spread the butter on crackers or bread.

2. Making Ice Cream

Collect the following ingredients:

1 cup milk
1/2 cup sugar
1/4 teaspoon salt
3 beaten egg yolks
1 tablespoon vanilla
2 cups whipping cream

In a saucepan, combine milk, sugar, salt, and egg yolks. Stir constantly over medium heat until bubbles appear around the edge of the pan. Cool mixture at room temperature. Stir in vanilla and whipping cream. Pour into an ice cream maker and follow the manufacturer's directions. (Recipe makes 1 quart of ice cream.)

3. Science Table Additions

Additions to the science table may include:

- pictures of dairy cows.
- books about milking cows and dairy animals.
- containers of grain, corn, and hay along with magnifying glasses.
- pictures of goats, sheep, and llamas.

Dramatic Play:

1. Ice Cream Shop

Clothes and props for an ice cream shop can be placed in the dramatic play area. Include items such as empty, clean ice cream pails and cartons, ice cream scoops, plastic parfait glasses and bowls, plastic spoons, empty ice cream cone boxes, napkins, aprons, and a cash register with play money. Prepare and display posters in the area that portray various ice cream products and flavors.

2. Dairy Farm

Turn the dramatic play center into a dairy farm where the children can pretend to do chores. Display pictures of farms and cows and provide overalls, boots, hats, pails, hoses, and other appropriate props.

3. Grocery Store—Dairy Department

Set up the dramatic play area to resemble the dairy department of a grocery store. Include props such as milk cartons, cottage cheese containers, yogurt cups, sour cream containers, ice cream pails and cartons, butter boxes, cheese packages, and a cash register. Display pictures of dairy foods.

Arts and Crafts:

1. **Buttermilk Chalk Pictures**

   Dip colored chalk into a small container of buttermilk or brush construction paper with buttermilk. Use the chalk to create designs on construction paper.

2. **Dairy Product Paint Containers**

   Use empty dairy product containers to hold paint for use at the art table or easel. Examples include milk cartons, yogurt cups, and cottage cheese containers.

3. **Whipped Soap Painting**

   The following mixture can be made to represent ice cream or cottage cheese. Mix one cup of Ivory Snow flakes with 1/2 cup of warm water in a bowl. The children can beat the mixture with a hand eggbeater until it is fluffy. Add more water, if necessary. Apply mixture with paint brushes or fingers to construction paper. For a variation, food coloring can be added to the paint mixture.

4. **Ice Cream Cone Sponge Painting**

   Cut sponges into shapes of ice cream cones and scoops of ice cream. Provide shallow trays of various colors of paints. Designs are created by dipping the sponge in the paint and then pressing it onto a piece of construction paper.

5. **Yogurt Cup Prints**

   Collect empty yogurt cups of various shapes and sizes. Wash them thoroughly. Prepare shallow trays of paint. Create designs by inverting a yogurt cup, dipping it into the paint, and then applying it to construction paper. Repeat the process as desired.

6. **Dairy Collage**

   Provide magazines that contain pictures of dairy products for the children to cut out. The pictures can be glued to a piece of construction paper, tagboard, or a paper plate for the children to create a collage.

Sensory:

Add to the sensory table:

- sand, scoops, and empty milk cartons.
- water and empty, clean yogurt and cottage cheese containers.
- cotton balls, spoons, ice cream scoops, bowls, and empty, clean ice cream pails.

Field Trips:

1. **The Grocery Store**

   Visit a grocery store and locate the dairy section. Look at the types of dairy products available.

2. **Ice Cream Shop**

   Take a trip to an ice cream shop. Count the flavors of ice cream available. Purchase a cone for each of the children.

3. **Dairy Farm**

   Visit a dairy farm. Ask the farmer to show the housing, equipment, and food supplies needed to care for dairy cows.

Math:

1. **Dairy Sort**

   Collect different types of food product containers, including dairy products. Place all of the containers in a basket. Encourage the children to sort out the containers representing dairy products from the other food product containers.

2. **Dairy Lids**

   Collect lids and caps from milk jugs. They can be recycled and used for game pieces, creating patterns, and counting activities.

3. **Favorite Ice Cream Graph**

The children can assist in making a graph of their favorite ice cream flavors. Begin by printing the caption, "Our Favorite Ice Cream Flavors," across the top of a piece of tagboard. Draw or paste pictures of different flavors of ice cream along the left-hand side of the tagboard. Each child's name or picture is placed next to the picture of his favorite ice cream flavor. The results of the graph should be shared with the children using math vocabulary words: most, more, fewer, least, etc. Display the graph for further reference.

Additional graphs could be made depicting the children's favorite flavors of yogurt, cheese, or milk.

Social Studies:

1. **Sharing a Treat**

Prepare a dairy food with the children and share it with another class, senior citizens group, or other community group.

2. **Role of the Dairy Farmer**

Invite a dairy farmer to the classroom to discuss his occupation. The equipment and tools used to farm could also be shown and discussed.

Group Time (games, language):

1. **Dairy Charts**

Print the caption, "Foods Made from Milk," across the top of a piece of tagboard. During group time, present the chart and record the children's responses. Display the chart and refer to it throughout the theme.

Additional language charts could be made about types of cheeses, ice cream, and yogurt.

2. **Cheese Tasting Party**

Cut various types of cheese into small slices or pieces. Place the cheese pieces on paper plates for the children to taste. Discuss types of cheeses, textures, flavors, and colors.

Cooking:

1. **Milk Shake**

For each shake, combine 1/2 cup of vanilla ice cream and one cup of milk in a blender. If desired, flavor the shake with one of the following: 1/2 cup fresh berries, 1/2 banana, two tablespoons of peanut butter, or two tablespoons chocolate syrup.

2. **Grilled Cheese Sandwich**

Assist the children in making cheese sandwiches. Provide plastic knives for the children to spread soft butter or margarine on the outside of sandwiches. Turn over and place a cheese slice between the two pieces of bread.

Under adult supervision, place the sandwiches on a heated skillet or electric grill until golden brown, turning once.

3. **Homemade Vanilla Pudding**

1/8 teaspoon salt
2 cups milk
2 slightly beaten egg yolks
1 tablespoon softened butter or margarine
2 teaspoons vanilla

Combine cornstarch, sugar, and salt in a medium saucepan. Stir in the milk. Over medium heat, cook and stir constantly until the mixture thickens and comes to a boil. Stir and boil one minute. In a small bowl, blend half of the hot mixture into the egg yolks. Pour the egg mixture back into the saucepan and cook until the mixture boils, stirring constantly. Remove the pan from the heat and add the butter and vanilla. Allow the pudding to cool slightly and spoon into a serving bowl or individual dishes. Refrigerate. (This recipe makes four servings.)

4. **Strawberry Yogurt Surprise**

3-oz. package strawberry-flavored gelatin
1 cup boiling water
1/2 cup cold water
1 cup strawberry yogurt

Dissolve gelatin in the boiling water. Stir in cold water. Chill until thickened but not set. Beat gelatin and fold in yogurt. Pour into serving dish. Refrigerate until firm. (This recipe makes four servings.)

Multimedia:

The following resources can be found in educational catalogs:

1. Raffi. "Down on Grandpa's Farm" on *One Light, One Sun* [record].

2. Raffi. "Corner Grocery Store" on *The Corner Grocery Store* [record].

3. Sharon, Lois, & Bram. "Did You Feed My Cow?" on *Smorgasbord* [record].

Books:

The following books can be used to complement the theme:

1. Ziegler, Sandra. (1987). *A Visit to the Dairy Farm*. Chicago: Children's Press.

2. Fowler, Allan. (1992). *Thanks to Cows*. Chicago: Children's Press.

3. Moncure, Jane. (1987). *Ice Cream Cows and Mitten Sheep*. Mankato, MN: Child's World, Inc.

4. Royston, Angela. (1990). *Cow*. New York: Franklin Watts, Inc.

5. Gibbons, Gail. (1985). *The Milk Makers*. New York: Macmillan Publishing Co.

6. Carrick, Donald. (1985). *Milk*. New York: Greenwillow Books.

7. Robbins, Ken. (1992). *Make Me a Peanut Butter Sandwich and a Glass of Milk*. New York: Scholastic, Inc.

8. Rice, Colleen. (1985). *What Was It Before It Was Ice Cream?* Mankato, MN: Child's World, Inc.

9. Asch, Frank. (1991). *Milk and Cookies*. New York: Putnam Publishing.

10. Modell, Frank. (1988). *Ice Cream Soup*. New York: Greenwillow.

11. Geringer, Laura. (1993). *The Cow Is Mooing Anyhow*. New York: Harper Collins.

12. Grossman, Bill. (1992). *Tommy at the Grocery Store Big Book*. New York: Harper Collins.

13. Peterson, Katherine. (1993). *Smallest Cow in the World*. New York: Harper Collins.

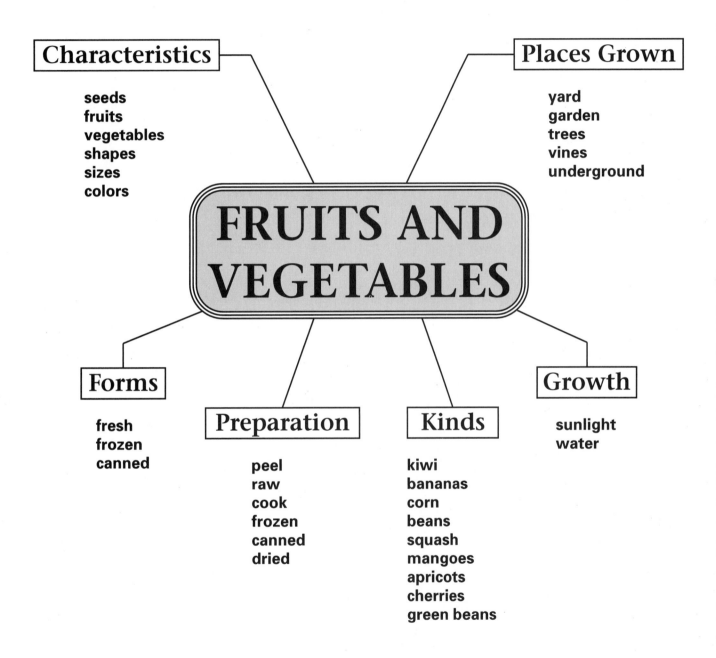

Characteristics

seeds
fruits
vegetables
shapes
sizes
colors

Places Grown

yard
garden
trees
vines
underground

FRUITS AND VEGETABLES

Forms

fresh
frozen
canned

Preparation

peel
raw
cook
frozen
canned
dried

Kinds

kiwi
bananas
corn
beans
squash
mangoes
apricots
cherries
green beans

Growth

sunlight
water

Theme Goals:

Through participating in the experiences provided by this theme, the children may learn:

1. Names of common fruits and vegetables.
2. Purposes of fruits and vegetables.
3. Places fruits and vegetables are grown.
4. Preparation of fruits and vegetables.
5. Tastes of fruits and vegetables.
6. Fruit or vegetable seeds.

Concepts for the Children to Learn:

1. There are many kinds of fruits and vegetables.
2. Fruits and vegetables come in many shapes, sizes, and colors.
3. Fruits and vegetables need sunlight and water to grow.
4. Fruits and vegetables can be bought fresh, frozen, or canned.
5. Some people grow fruits and vegetables in gardens.
6. Fruits and vegetables have different names.
7. Most fruits and vegetables can be eaten raw or cooked.
8. Some fruits and vegetables we eat with skin; some we need to peel first.
9. Some fruits have seeds.

Vocabulary:

1. **fruit**—usually a sweet-tasting part of a plant.
2. **vegetable**—part of a plant that can be eaten.
3. **garden**—ground used to grow plants.
4. **produce**—agriculture products such as fruits and vegetables.
5. **vine**—plant with long, slender stem.
6. **cooked**—prepare food by heating.
7. **frozen**—chilled or refrigerated to make solid.
8. **seeds**—part of a plant used for growing a new crop and is edible in some plants (sunflower, pumpkin).
9. **roots**—part of a plant that grows downward into the soil and is edible in some plants (potatoes, turnips, radishes, onions, and carrots).
10. **soil**—portion of earth; dirt used for growing.
11. **sprout**—to begin to grow.
12. **stems**—part of a plant used for transporting food and water and is edible in some plants (celery).

Bulletin Board

The purpose of this bulletin board is to observe the growth of a lima bean seed. To prepare the bulletin board, place a moist paper towel in a small plastic bag and place a lima bean on top of the towel for each child. Staple each bag to the bulletin board as illustrated; place each child's name by his bag. Sprouting will occur faster if seeds have been pre-soaked overnight. Additional watering may be needed throughout the unit.

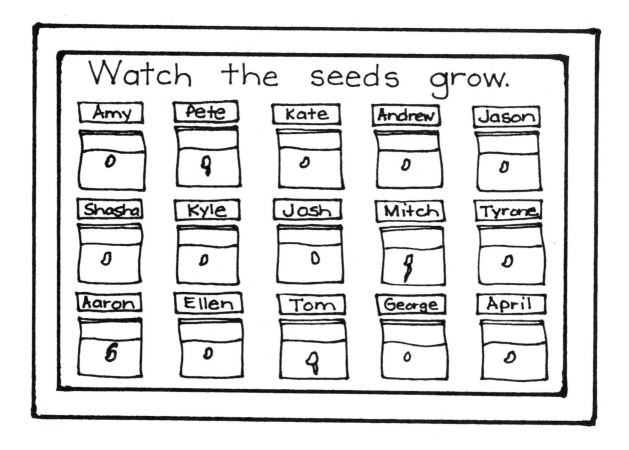

Parent Letter

Dear Parents,

Hello again! We hope that everyone in your family is healthy and happy. Speaking of health, we are starting a new unit on fruits and vegetables. Through the experiences planned for this unit, the children will become aware of many fruits and vegetables and how they are grown. Also, they will discover how many fruits and vegetables taste.

At School

Some of the many fun-filled learning activities scheduled for this unit are:

- planting lima bean seeds to sprout. Take a look at our bulletin board this week.
- playing the role of a gardener/farmer in the dramatic play area.
- matching pictures of vegetables to where they are grown (trees, vines, underground, etc.).
- having a fruit and vegetable tasting party during snack.
- visiting a produce section at the grocery store.
- listening to a story called *What Was It Before It Was Orange Juice?* by Jane Belk Moncure.

At Home

There are many ways that you can integrate concepts included in this unit into your family life. To help develop memory and language skills, ask your child which vegetables or fruit he tried during the week. Then let your child help you prepare them at home. Cooking often tempts a child to try new foods. Also, here is a great dip recipe we will be making for snack on Tuesday that you may want to make at home also.

Vegetable Dip

1 cup yogurt
1 cup mayonnaise
1 tablespoon dill weed
1 teaspoon seasoned salt

Mix all ingredients and chill. Serve with fresh raw vegetables.

We still need two more helpers to assist us with our field trip on Thursday to the grocery store. Let me know if you are available. The children enjoy having parents join in our activities.

Enjoy your child!

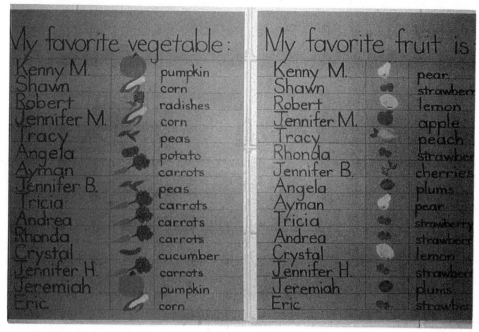

Trying different fruits and vegetables and listing favorites is a good activity.

Music:

1. **"The Vegetable Garden"**
   (Sing to the tune of "Mulberry Bush")

   Here we go 'round the vegetable garden,
   The vegetable garden, the vegetable garden,
   Here we go round the vegetable garden,
   So early in the morning.

   Other verses:
   This is the way we pull the weeds…
   This is the way we water the plants…
   This is the way we eat the vegetables…

2. **"Vegetables"**
   (Sing to the tune "Mary Had a Little Lamb")

   I'm a tomato, red and round,
   Red and round, red and round.
   I'm a tomato, red and round,
   Seated on the ground.

   I'm a corn stalk, tall and straight,
   Tall and straight, tall and straight.
   I'm a corn stalk, tall and straight
   And I taste just great.

Fingerplays:

MY GARDEN

This is my garden
   (extend one hand forward, palm up)
I'll rake it with care
   (make raking motion on palm with three
   fingers of other hand)
And then some seeds
   (planting motion)
I'll plant in there.
The sun will shine
   (make circle with arms)
And the rain will fall
   (let fingers flutter down to lap)
And my garden will blossom
   (cup hand together, extend upward slowly)
And grow straight and tall.

DIG A LITTLE HOLE

Dig a little hole.
   (dig)
Plant a little seed.
   (drop seed)
Pour a little water.
   (pour)

Pull a little weed.
    (pull and throw)
Chase a little bug.
    (chasing motion with hands)
Heigh-ho, there he goes.
    (shade eyes)
Give a little sunshine
    (circle arms over head)
Grow a little bean!
    (hands grow upward)

APPLE TREE

Way up high in the apple tree
    (hold arms up high)
Two little apples smiled at me.
    (look at two hands up high)
I shook that tree as hard as I could.
    (shake arms)
Down came the apples,
    (arms fall)
Mmm, were they good!
    (rub tummy)

BANANAS

Bananas are my favorite fruit.
    (make fists as if holding banana)
I eat one every day.
    (hold up one finger)
I always take one with me
    (act as if putting one in pocket)
When I go out to play.
    (wave good-bye)
It gives me lots of energy
    (make a muscle)
To jump around and run.
    (move arms as if running)
Bananas are my favorite fruit.
    (rub tummy)
To me they're so much fun!
    (point to self and smile)

VEGETABLES AND FRUITS

The food we like to eat that grows
On vines and bushes and trees.
Are vegetables and fruits my friends
Like cherries, grapes, and peas.
Apples and oranges and peaches are fruits
And so are tangerines,
Lettuce and carrots are vegetables,
Like squash and beans.

Science:

1. **Cut and Draw**

   Cut out or draw many different fruits and vegetables from tagboard or construction paper scraps. Also make a tree, a vine, and some soil. Have children classify the fruit to where it's grown—on a tree, on vines, or underground.

2. **Tasting Center**

   Cut small pieces of various fruits and set up a tasting center. Encourage the children to taste and compare different fruits and vegetables.

3. **Tasting Party**

   Plan a vegetable tasting party. Cut small pieces of vegetables. Also, have children taste raw vegetables compared to the same vegetable cooked.

4. **Identify by Smelling**

   Place one each of several fruits and vegetables in small cups and cover with aluminum foil. Punch a small hole in the top of the aluminum foil. Then have the children smell the cups and try to identify each fruit or vegetable.

5. **Growing a Seed**

   Give each child a plastic sealable bag, a moistened paper towel, and a lima bean. Demonstrate how to place the bean in the paper towel and close bag. After the children have finished planting their beans, place each child's bag on a bulletin board. Check the bulletin board on a daily basis to see when the seed sprouts.

6. **Carrot Tops in Water**

   Cut off the top of a carrot and place it in a shallow dish of water. Observe what happens day to day. Given time, the top of the carrot should sprout.

7. Colored Celery Stalks

Place celery stalks into water colored with food coloring. Observe what happens to the leaves of celery.

Dramatic Play:

Grocery Store

Plan a grocery store containing many plastic fruits and vegetables, a cash register, grocery bags, and play money if available. The children can take turns being a produce clerk, cashier, and price tagger.

Arts and Crafts:

1. Fruit and Vegetable Collage

Make a fruit and vegetable collage. Have children draw or cut their favorite fruits and vegetables from magazines and paste on paper.

2. Seeds

Save several seeds from fruits and vegetables for the children to make a seed collage. When seeds are securely glued, children can also paint them if desired. The collage can be secured to a bulletin board.

3. Cutting Vegetable and Fruit Shapes

Cut easel paper into a different shape of fruit or vegetable every day.

4. Mold with Playdough

The children can mold and create fruits and vegetables out of clay and playdough. Another option would be to color and scent the play-dough. Examples might include orange-smelling orange, lemon-smelling yellow, banana-smelling yellow.

5. Potato Prints

Cut potatoes in half. The children can dip in paints and stamp the potatoes on a large sheet of paper.

6. Paint with Celery Leaves

Mix some thin tempera paint. Use celery leaves as a painting tool.

Sensory:

Preparing Fruits and Vegetables

Wash vegetables and fruits to prepare for eating at snack time.

Large Muscle:

Place hoes, shovels, rakes, and watering cans around the outdoor sand area.

Field Trips:

1. Grocery Store

Take a trip to the grocery store to visit the produce department. Ask the clerk to show the children how the food is delivered.

2. Visiting a Farm

Visit a farm. Ask the farmer to show the children the fruits and vegetables grown on the farm.

3. Visit a Farmers' Market

Visit a farmers' market. Purchase fruits and vegetables that can be used for snacks.

4. Visit an Orchard

Visit an apple or fruit orchard. Observe how the fruit is grown. If possible, pick some fruit to bring back to the classroom.

Math:

1. Fruit and Vegetable Match

Cut out various fruits and vegetables from a magazine. Trace their shapes onto tagboard. Have children match the fruit or vegetable to the correct shape on the tagboard.

2. Seriation

Make five sizes of each vegetable or fruit you want to use. Have children place in order from smallest to largest, or largest to smallest.

3. Measuring

The children can measure their bean sprouts. Maintain a small chart of their measurements.

4. Parts and Wholes

Cut apples in half at snack time to introduce the concepts of parts and whole.

5. Grouping Pictures

Cut pictures of fruits and vegetables for the children to sort according to color, size, and shape.

Social Studies:

1. Field Trip to a Garden

Plan a field trip to a large garden. Point out different fruits and vegetables. If possible, have the children pull radishes and carrots.

2. Hang Pictures

On a bulletin board in the classroom hang pictures of fruits and vegetables.

3. Fruit and Vegetable Book

The children can make a fruit and vegetable book. Possible titles include "My favorite fruit is," "My favorite vegetable is," "I would like to grow," and "I would most like to cook." The children can paste pictures or adhere stickers to the individual pages.

Group Time (games, language):

1. Carrot, Carrot, Corn

Play "Duck, Duck Goose," but substitute "Carrot, Carrot, Corn."

2. Hot Potato

The children sit in a circle and the teacher gives one child a potato. Teacher then plays lively music and the children pass potato around the circle. When the music suddenly stops, the child with the potato must stand up and say the name of a fruit or vegetable. Encourage children to think of a fruit or vegetable that hasn't been named yet. Play the game until almost all fruits and vegetables have been named.

Cooking:

1. Vegetable Dip

1 cup plain yogurt
1 cup mayonnaise
1 tablespoon dill weed
1 teaspoon seasoned salt

Mix all the ingredients together and chill. Serve with fresh raw vegetables.

2. Ants on a Log

Cut celery into pieces and spread with peanut butter. Top with raisins, coconut, or grated carrots. (Celery is difficult for younger children to chew.)

3. Applesauce

4 apples
1 tablespoon water
2 tablespoons brown sugar or honey

Wash the apples and cut into small pieces. Dip the pieces into water and roll in brown sugar or honey. Serves 8.

4. Banana Rounds

4 medium bananas
1/2 cup yogurt
3 tablespoons honey
1/8 teaspoon nutmeg
1/8 teaspoon cinnamon
1/4 cup wheat germ

The children can participate by peeling the bananas and slicing into "rounds." Measure the spices, wheat germ, and honey. Blend this mixture with yogurt and bananas. Chill prior to serving. Serves 8.

5. Middle East Date and Banana Dessert

4 ounces (1 cup) pitted dates, cut up
2 bananas, thinly sliced
2 to 3 teaspoons finely shredded lemon peel
1/2 cup half and half
sliced almonds (optional)

Alternate layers of dates and bananas in serving dish or dessert dishes. Sprinkle with lemon peel. Pour half and half over top. Cover and refrigerate at least 4 hours. Just before serving sprinkle with almonds. Makes 3 to 4 servings.

Source: *Betty Crocker's International Cookbook.* (1980). New York: Random House.

6. Finnish Strawberry Shake

20 fresh strawberries
4 cups milk
3 tablespoons sugar

Wash strawberries and remove stems. Cut strawberries into small pieces. Combine milk, sugar, and strawberries in a large mixing bowl or blender. Beat with an eggbeater or blend for 2 minutes. Pour strawberry shakes into individual glasses. Makes 4 to 8 servings.

Variation: Raspberries or other sweet fruit may be used instead.

7. Banana Sandwiches

1/2 or 1 banana per child
peanut butter

Peel the bananas and slice them in half lengthwise. Spread peanut butter on one half of the banana and top with the other half.

COOKING VOCABULARY

The following vocabulary words can be introduced through cooking experiences:

bake	garnish	scrape
beat	grate	scrub
boil	grease	shake
broil	grill	shread
brown	grind	sift
chop	heat	simmer
cool	knead	spread
core	marinate	sprinkle
cream	measure	squeeze
cube	mince	stir
cut	mix	strain
dice	pare	stuff
dip	peel	tear
drain	pit	toast
freeze	pour	whip
frost	roast	
fry	roll	

Multimedia:

The following resources can be found in preschool educational catalogs:

1. Palmer, Hap. *Learning Basic Skills Through Music—Health and Safety* [record]. #EA AR526R.

2. Avni, Fran. *Artichokes & Brussels Sprouts* [record]. Alphabetical.

Books:

The following books can be used to complement the theme:

1. Moncure, Jane Belk. (1985). *What Was It Before It Was Orange Juice?* Chicago: Children's Press.

2. *Eating the Alphabet: Fruits and Vegetables A to Z.* (1989). San Diego: Harcourt Brace Jovanovich.

3. Robinson, Fay. (1992). *We Love Fruit.* Chicago: Children's Press.

4. de Bourgoing, Pascale. (1991). *Fruit.* New York: Scholastic, Inc.

5. Wexler, Jerome. (1990). *Flower Fruit Seeds.* New York: Simon and Schuster.

6. Watts, Barrie. (1990). *Tomato.* Morristown, NJ: Silver Burdett Press.

7. Politi, Leo. (1993). *Three Stalks of Corn.* New York: Macmillan.

8. Berger, Thomas. (1990). *The Mouse and the Potato.* Edinburgh, Scotland: Floris Books.

9. Ehlert, Lois. (1987). *Growing Vegetable Soup.* San Diego, CA: Harcourt Brace Jovanovich.

10. Weiss, Ellen. (1989). *Oh Beans! Starring Wax Beans.* Mahwah, NJ: Troll.

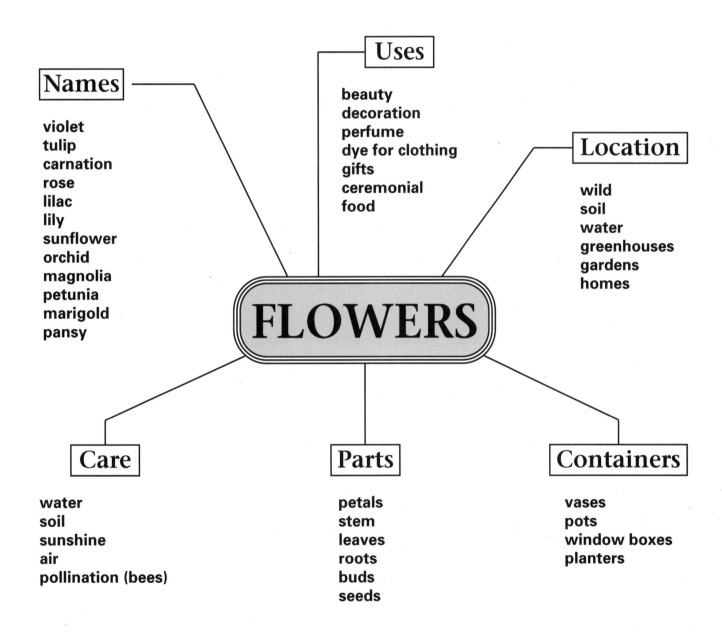

Names

violet
tulip
carnation
rose
lilac
lily
sunflower
orchid
magnolia
petunia
marigold
pansy

Uses

beauty
decoration
perfume
dye for clothing
gifts
ceremonial
food

Location

wild
soil
water
greenhouses
gardens
homes

FLOWERS

Care

water
soil
sunshine
air
pollination (bees)

Parts

petals
stem
leaves
roots
buds
seeds

Containers

vases
pots
window boxes
planters

Theme Goals:

Through participating in the experiences provided by this theme, the children may learn:

1. Parts of the flower.

2. Flowers have names.

3. Places flowers grow.

4. Uses of flowers.

5. Containers that hold flowers.

6. Care of flowers.

Concepts for the Children to Learn:

1. A flower is a plant.

2. Flowers add beauty to our world.

3. Flowers can be used for decoration.

4. Most flowers have a smell.

5. Vases, pots, window boxes, and planters are all flower containers.

6. Flowers need soil, water, sunshine, and air to grow.

7. Sometimes flowers are given to people for special reasons, such as holidays, birthdays, or if someone goes to the hospital.

Vocabulary:

1. **flower**—part of a plant that blossoms.

2. **petal**—colored part of a flower.

3. **seed**—produces a new plant.

4. **stem**—the trunk of the plant.

5. **leaves**—growth from the stem.

6. **greenhouse**—a glass house for growing plants.

7. **root**—the part of the plant that usually grows down into the soil.

Bulletin Board

The purpose of this bulletin board is to develop color matching skills, as well as foster the correspondence of sets to written numerals. A math skills bulletin board can be created by cutting large numerals out of tagboard. Color each number a different color. Next, create tulips out of tagboard. The number will be dependent upon the maturity of the children. Color one tulip the same color as the numeral one. Color two tulips the same color as the numeral two. Continue with the numerals three and four. The children can hang the appropriate number of tulips on the bulletin board next to each numeral. The children can also match the colored tulips next to the corresponding colored numeral to make this activity self-correcting.

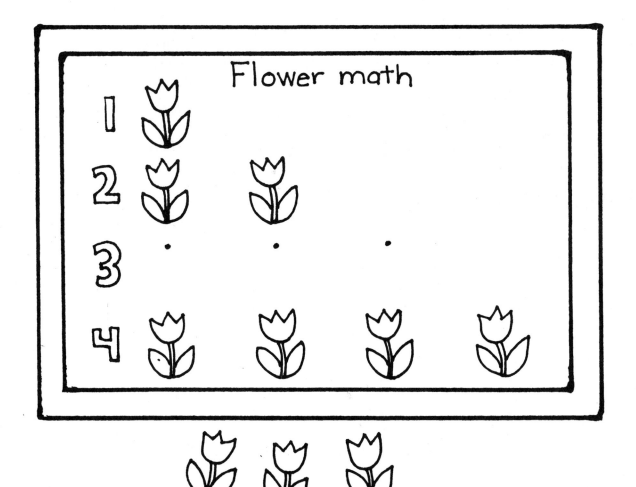

Parent Letter

Dear Parents,

Hello! As spring arrives and all the flowers begin to bloom, we will begin a unit on flowers. Through this unit the children will learn about the care, uses, and parts of a flowering plant.

At School

Some of the learning experiences planned to help the children make discoveries about flowers include:

- listening to the story, *Dandelion,* by Ladislav Svatos.
- observing and measuring the growth of various flowers.
- visiting a floral shop.
- playing a flower beanbag toss game.

At Home

You can integrate the concepts included in this unit into your home in many ways. If you are planning to plant a garden in your yard this spring, let your child help you. It might even be fun to section off a small part of your garden for your child to grow flowers and care for them. Another activity would be to examine the plants and flowers you have growing in your house. Also, let your child send flowers to someone special.

To develop language skills, we will be learning this fingerplay in school. Let your child teach it to you.

Daisies

One, two, three, four, five
    (pop up fingers, one at a time)
Yellow daisies all alive.
Here they are all in a row.
    (point to fingers standing)
The sun and the rain will help them grow.
    (make a circle with fingers, flutter fingers for rain)

Enjoy your child!

Children learn science concepts by growing flowers.

Music:

"Flowers"
   (Sing to the tune of "Pop! Goes the Weasel")

   All around the forest ground
   There's flowers everywhere.
   There's pink, yellow, and purple, too.
   Here's one for you.

Fingerplays:

MY GARDEN

   This is my garden
      (extend one hand forward, palm up)
   I'll rake it with care
      (raking motion with fingers)
   And then some flower seeds
      (planting motion)

   I'll plant in right there.
   The sun will shine
      (make circle with hands)
   And the rain will fall
      (let fingers flutter down to lap)
   And my garden will blossom
      (cup hands together, extend upward slowly)
   And grow straight and tall.

DAISIES

   One, two, three, four, five
      (pop up fingers, one at a time)
   Yellow daisies all alive.
   Here they are all in a row.
      (point to fingers standing)
   The sun and the rain will help them grow.
      (make a circle with fingers, flutter fingers for rain)

FLOWER PLAY

   If I were a little flower
   Sleeping underneath the ground,
      (curl up)
   I'd raise my head and grow and grow
      (raise head and begin to grow)
   And stretch my arms and grow and grow
      (stretch arms)
   And nod my head and say,
      (nod head)
   "I'm glad to see you all today."

Science:

1. **Flowers**

   Place a variety of flowers on the science table. Encourage the children to compare the color, shape, size, and smell of each flower.

2. **Planting Seeds**

   Plant flower seeds in a styrofoam cup. Save the seed packages and mount on a piece of tagboard. Place this directly behind the containers on the science table. Encourage the children to compare their plants. When the plant starts growing, compare the seed packages to the plant growth.

3. **Carnation**

Place a white carnation in a vase containing water with red food coloring added. Watch the tips of the carnation petals gradually change colors. Repeat the activity using other flowers and colors of water.

4. **Observing and Weighing Bulbs**

Collect flower bulbs and place in the science table. Encourage the children to observe the similarities and differences. A balance scale can also be added.

5. **Microscopes**

Place petals from a flower under a microscope for the children to observe.

Dramatic Play:

1. **Garden**

Aprons, small garden tools, a tin of soil, seeds, watering cans, pots, and vases can all be provided. Pictures of flowers with names on them can be hung in the classroom.

2. **Gardener**

Gather materials for a gardener prop box. Include gloves, seed packets, sun hat, hoe, stakes for marking, watering cans, etc.

3. **Flower Shop**

In the dramatic play area, set up a flower shop complete with plastic flowers, boxes, containers, watering cans, misting bottle, and cash register. Artificial corsages would also be a fun addition.

4. **Flower Arranging**

Artificial flowers and containers can be placed in the dramatic play area. The children can make centerpieces for the lunch table. Also, a centerpiece can be made for the science table, the lobby, and the secretary, director, or principal.

Arts and Crafts:

1. **Muffin Cup Flowers**

For younger children, prepare shapes of flowers and leaves. The older children may be able to do this themselves. Attach the stems and leaves to muffin tin liners. Add a small amount of perfume to the flower for interest.

2. **Collage**

Cut pictures of flowers from seed catalogs. With these flowers, create a collage.

3. **Easel**

Cut easel paper into flower shapes.

4. **Seed Collages**

Place a pan containing a variety of seeds in the middle of the art table. In addition, supply glue and paper for the children to form a collage.

5. **Egg Carton Flowers**

Cut the sections of an egg container apart. Attach pipe cleaners for stems and decorate with watercolor markers.

6. **Flower Mobile**

Bring in a tree branch and hang from the classroom ceiling. Let the children make flowers and hang them on the branch for decoration.

7. **Paper Plate Flowers**

Provide snack-sized paper plates, markers, crayons, and colored construction paper. The children may use these materials to create a flower.

Sensory:

Add to the sensory table:

- soil and plastic flowers
- water and watering cans

Field Trips/Resource People:

1. **Florist**

   Arrange to visit a local floral shop. Observe the different kinds of flowers. Then watch the florist design a bouquet or corsage.

2. **Walk**

   Walk around the neighborhood observing different types and colors of flowers.

Math:

1. **Flower Growth**

   Prepare sequence cards representing flowers at various stages of growth. Encourage the children to sequence them.

2. **Flower Match**

   Cut pictures of flowers from magazines or seed catalogs. If desired, mount the pictures. The children can match them by kind, size, color, and shape.

3. **Measuring Seed Growth**

   Plant several types of seeds. At determined intervals, measure the growth of various plants and flowers. Maintain a chart comparing the growth.

Group Time (games, language):

Hide the Flower

Choose one child to look for the flower. Ask him to cover his eyes. Ask another child to hide a flower. After the flower is hidden and the child returns to the group, instruct the first child to uncover his eyes and find the flower. Clues can be provided. For example, if the child aproaches the area where the flower is hidden, the remainder of the children can clap their hands.

Cooking:

1. **Fruit Candy**

   Some fruits start with a flower. Discuss which of the following fruits begin with a flower from the ingredients below.

   1 pound dried figs
   1 pound dried apricots
   1/2 pound dates
   2 cups walnuts
   1/2 cup raisins
   1/2 cup coarsely chopped walnuts

   Put fruits and 2 cups of walnuts through a food grinder. Mix in the 1/2 cup of chopped walnuts and press into a buttered 9-inch x 13-inch pan. Chill and enjoy!

2. **China—Egg Flower Soup**

   Watch an egg turn into a flower. Chinese cooks say that the cooked shreds of egg afloat in this soup look like flower petals.

   1 tablespoon cornstarch
   2 tablespoons cold water
   1 egg
   3 cups clear canned chicken broth
   1 teaspoon salt
   1 teaspoon chopped scallion or parsley
     (optional)

   Put the cornstarch into a small bowl and gradually add water, stirring it with a fork until you no longer see any lumps. Break the egg into another small bowl and beat it with the fork. Pour the broth into the saucepan. Bring it to a boil over high heat. Add the salt. Give the cornstarch and water mixture a quick stir with the fork. Add it to the soup. Stir the soup with a spoon until it thickens and becomes clear (about one minute). Slowly pour the beaten egg into the soup. The egg will cook in the hot soup and form shreds. When all the egg has been added, stir once. Turn off the heat. Pour the soup into 4 soup bowls. Top if desired with chopped scallion or parsley for decorations.

   Source: Touff, Terry, & Ratner, Marilyn. (1974). *Many Hands Cooking*. New York: Thomas Y. Crowell Company.

3. **Dandelion Salad**

6 cups young dandelion leaves, picked before flower blossoms
croutons, hard-boiled eggs, vegetables (optional)
dressing

Thoroughly wash the dandelion greens, removing stems and roots. Tear the leaves into small pieces and place in bowls. Add optional ingredients. Toss with salad dressing.

Multimedia:

The following resources can be found in educational catalogs:

1. Follman, Ilene, & Jackson, Helen. "Dandelion Seed" on *Science in a Nutshell* [record].

2. *Daisy Quest* [Mac software, PK–2]. Great Wave.

Books:

The following books can be used to complement the theme:

1. Braithwaite, Althea. (1988). *Flowers*. Chicago: Dearborn Financial Publishing, Inc.

2. Butterfield, Moira. (1992). *Flower*. New York: Simon and Schuster Trade.

3. Wexler, Jerome. (1990). *Flowers Fruits Seeds*. New York: Simon and Schuster Trade.

4. Ehlert, Lois. (1992). *Planting a Rainbow*. San Diego: Harcourt Brace Jovanovich.

5. Turner, Ann, & Blake, Robert J. (1992). *Rainflowers*. New York: Harper Collins Children's Books.

6. Jordan, Helene J. (1992). *How a Seed Grows*. New York: Crowell Junior Books.

7. Demi. (1990). *The Empty Pot*. New York: Henry Holt.

8. Fowler, Allan. (1993). *What's Your Favorite Flower?* Children's Books.

9. dePaola, Tomie. (1988). *The Legend of the Indian Paintbrush*. New York: G. P. Putnam's Sons.

THEME

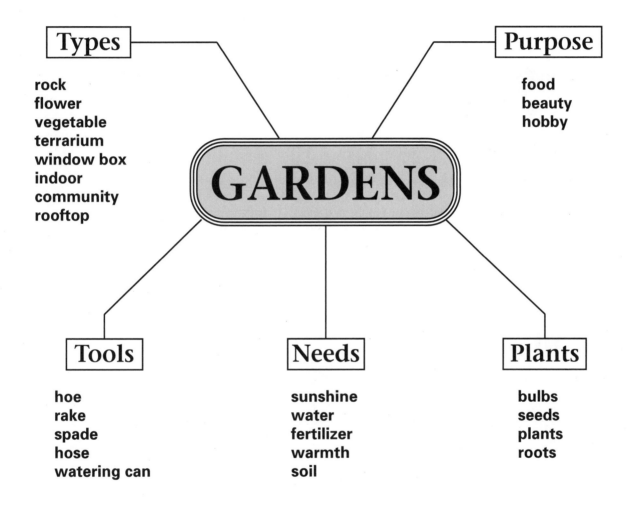

Types

rock
flower
vegetable
terrarium
window box
indoor
community
rooftop

Purpose

food
beauty
hobby

GARDENS

Tools

hoe
rake
spade
hose
watering can

Needs

sunshine
water
fertilizer
warmth
soil

Plants

bulbs
seeds
plants
roots

Theme Goals:

Through participating in the experiences provided by this theme, the children may learn:

1. Purposes of gardens.

2. Types of gardens.

3. Tools used for gardening.

4. Care of gardens.

5. Types of plants grown in a garden.

Concepts for the Children to Learn:

1. Plants are living things.

2. Plants need sunshine, water, soil, fertilizer, and warmth to grow.

3. Gardens produce food and beautiful flowers.

4. We plant gardens by placing bulbs, seeds, plants, or roots in the ground.

5. Weeds are plants that do not bear fruit. They take water and food from our garden plants.

6. Fruits, vegetables, and flowers can be planted in our gardens.

Vocabulary:

1. **bulb**—a type of seed.

2. **flower**—part of the plant that has colored petals.

3. **garden**—a place to grow plants.

4. **greenhouse**—building for growing plants and flowers.

5. **leaf**—flat green part of a plant.

6. **rake**—a tool with teeth or prongs.

7. **soil**—top of the ground.

8. **root**—part of the plant that grows into the ground.

9. **seed**—part of the plant from which a new plant will grow.

10. **stem**—part of the plant that holds the leaves and flowers.

11. **vegetable**—a plant that can be eaten.

12. **weed**—plant that is not needed.

Bulletin Board

The purpose of this bulletin board is to foster visual discrimination skills. To prepare the bulletin board, construct five or six watering cans out of tagboard. Color each one a different color with felt-tip markers and hang on the bulletin board. Attach a string to each watering can. Next, construct the same number of small rakes out of tagboard. Color each one using the same colors you used for the watering cans. Attach a push pin to the top of each rake. The children can match each watering can to the corresponding colored rake by winding the string around the correct push pin.

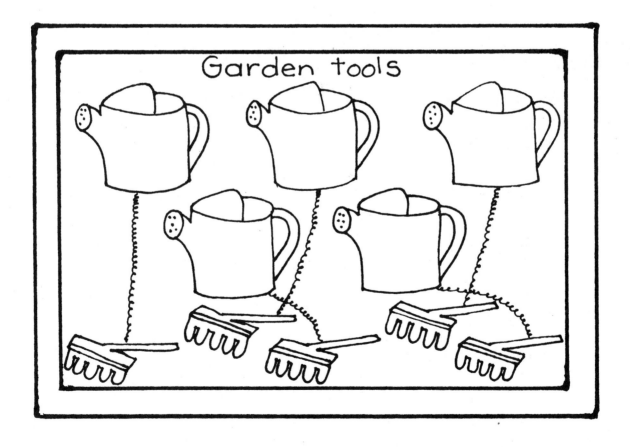

Parent Letter

Dear Parents,

"Mary, Mary, quite contrary, how does your garden grow?" That familiar nursery rhyme sums up our next theme—gardens! We will be exploring flower and vegetable gardens, as well as finding out about the work involved in planning and maintaining gardens and garden tools.

At School

Some of the learning experiences planned to foster concepts related to gardens include:

- a flower shop set up in the dramatic play area.
- dramatizing the story of *The Big Turnip*.
- preparing a section of our play yard for a garden. The children will help decide which seeds to plant.
- mud in the sensory table.

At Home

If you have a garden, ask your child to help you water, weed, and care for it. If you don't have a garden, take a walk and observe how many plants you can find that are cared for by people. What are the plants? How are they cared for?

Cut the tops of carrots off 1/4 inch from the stem to make a carrot-top garden. Place carrot tops in a shallow pie tin and pour 1/4 inch of water in the tin. Soon roots will appear, the greens will grow, and your child will be able to observe the growth.

Enjoy your child!

Watching a garden grow is a long-term science experience.

Music:

"A Little Seed"
(Sing to the tune of "I'm a Little Teapot")

Here's a little seed in the dark, dark ground.
Out comes the warm sun, yellow and round.
Down comes the rain, wet and slow.
Up comes the little seed, grow, grow, grow!

Fingerplays:

SEEDS

Some little seeds have parachutes
To carry them around
   (cup hand downward)
The wind blows them swish, swish, swish.
   (flip fingers outward from parachute)

Then gently lays them on the ground.
   (let hand gently float down and rest on lap)

RELAXING FLOWERS

Five little flowers standing in the sun
   (hold up five fingers)
See their heads nodding, bowing one by one?
   (bend fingers several times)
Down, down, down comes the gentle rain
   (raise hands, wiggle fingers, and lower arms
   to simulate falling rain)
And the five little flowers lift their heads up
again!
   (hold up five fingers)

HOW IT HAPPENS

A muddy hump,
   (make a fist using both hands)
A small green lump,
   (poke up thumbs together as one)
Two leaves and then
Two leaves again
   (raise forefinger of each hand from fist, then
   middle fingers)
And shooting up, a stem and cup.
   (put elbows, forearms, and hands together,
   fingers slightly curved)
One last shower,
   (rain movements with spread arms and
   fingers)
Then a flower.
   (elbows, forearms together with hands wide
   apart, palms up)

LITTLE FLOWERS

The sun comes out and shines so bright
   (join hands over head in circle)
Then we have a shower.
   (wiggle fingers coming down)
The little bud pushes with all its might
   (one hand in fist; other hand clasped over,
   move hands up slowly)
And soon we have a flower.
   (join thumbs and spread fingers for flower)

MR. CARROT

Nice Mr. Carrot
Makes curly hair.
   (hand on head)

His head grows underneath the ground,
   (bob head)
His feet up in the air.
   (raise feet)
And early in the morning
I find him in his bed
   (close eyes, lay head on hands)
And give his feet a great big pull
   (stretch legs out)
And out comes his head.

Science:

1. **Growing Grass**

   Germinate grass seeds by placing a damp sponge in a pie tin of water and sprinkling seeds on the sponge. The children will notice tiny sprouts after a few days. Experiment by putting one sponge in the freezer, one near a heat source, and one in a dark closet. Discuss what happens to each group of seeds.

2. **Plants Contain Water**

   Cut off 1/4 inch from the bottom of a celery stalk. Fill a clear vase with water containing food coloring. Place the celery stalk in the vase. Encourage the children to observe color changes in the celery stalk. This activity can be repeated using a white carnation.

3. **Planting Seeds**

   Purchase bean and radish seeds. If space permits, plant outdoors. Otherwise, place soil in planters indoors. Plant the seeds with the children. Identify the plants by pasting the seed packages on the planters. This will help the children to recognize the plants as they emerge from the soil.

4. **The Science Table**

   Place a magnifying glass with different types of seeds and bulbs on the science table. During the week add fresh flowers, plant leaves, and dried plants.

5. **Rooting a Sweet Potato**

   To root a sweet potato in water, push toothpicks halfway into the potato. Then place the potato in a glass of water with the toothpicks resting on the top rim. Make sure the end of the potato is immersed in water. Place the glass where it will receive adequate light. Maintain the water level so that the bottom of the potato is always immersed. Note that in a few weeks roots will grow out of the sides and bottom of the potato, and leaves will grow out of the top. The plant can be left in the water or replanted in soil. This activity provides the children an opportunity to observe root growth.

6. **Worm Farm**

   Collect the following materials: large clear jar with a wide mouth, soil, earthworms, gravel, and food for worms (lettuce, cornmeal, cereals). Place gravel and soil in the jar. Add the worms. Add food on the top of the dirt and keep the soil moist, but not wet. Tape black construction paper around outside of jar. The paper can be temporarily removed to observe the worms and see their tunnels.

Dramatic Play:

1. **Flower Shop**

   Introduce a flower shop by gathering plastic flowers and plants. If desired, flowers can be made from tissue paper and pipe cleaners. Collect different kinds of vases and also styrofoam or sponge blocks so the children can make flower arrangements. A cash register, aprons, money, and sacks can also be provided to encourage play.

2. **Gardening Center**

   Gather tools, gloves, hats, seeds, and plastic flowers or plants. The children can pretend to plant and grow seeds. Provide seed catalogs and order blanks for children to choose seeds to order.

3. **Fruit Stand**

   Set up a fruit stand by using plastic fruits and vegetables. Aprons, a cash register, market baskets or bags, and play money can also be used to encourage play. The children can take turns being the owner and the shopper.

4. **Sandbox**

The children can experiment with gardening tools in the sandbox.

Arts and Crafts:

1. **Collage**

Make collages using all types of seeds and beans. This activity can also be used by cutting pictures from seed catalogs.

2. **Leaf Rubbings**

Take the children on a leaf walk. The children choose a couple of large leaves to bring back to school. Place the leaves between two sheets of paper and rub with flat, large crayons across the top sheet of paper.

3. **Stencils**

Cut stencils out of tagboard of various-shaped leaves or vegetables. Laminate the stencils. The children can use crayons, pencils, or marking pens to make the leaf or vegetable outlines. These stencils can be used as the front of the "soup and salad" party invitations listed under social studies activities.

4. **Decorating Vases**

Collect tin cans or milk cartons for the children to use as vases. If cans are used, file the sharp edges or cover them with masking tape. The children can decorate the containers with colored paper, gift wrapping paper, or wallpaper. Greeting cards may also be useful for this activity.

Sensory:

1. **Sensory Activities**

In the sensory table place:

- soil
- seeds
- plastic plants
- beans
- measuring cups
- balance scales
- worms
- miniature garden tools
- cut grass or hay

2. **Fill and Guess**

After showing and discussing several kinds of fruits or vegetables with children, place the fruits or vegetables in a bag. Individually let children reach in and touch one item. See if they can guess what it is before pulling it out of the bag. Older children may also be able to describe the item.

Large Muscle:

Leaf Jumping

This is an active skill game that can be played indoors or outdoors. Cut out large cardboard leaves and arrange them in an irregular line, as they might appear on a stem. The closer they are together, the harder the game will be. Beginning at one end, each player tries to jump over the leaves without touching them. Older children may try to skip or hop over the leaves.

Field Trips/Resource People:

1. **Field Trips**

Take a field trip to:

- a flower garden
- a vegetable garden
- a flower shop
- a farmers' market
- a greenhouse
- a conservatory
- a park
- the produce section of a grocery store
- a natural food store

2. **Resource People**

- gardeners
- florist to demonstrate flower arranging

Math:

1. **Sorting Beans**

   Mix together several shapes and colors of large, dried beans. The children can sort the beans by size and color.

2. **Inchworm Measuring**

   A good introduction for this activity is the story *Inch by Inch* by Leo Lionni. Cut 2 or 3 dozen inchworms out of felt. Then cut out flowers of various heights—with long or short stems. Encourage the children to place worms along stem from bottom to top of flower. How many inchworms tall is each flower? After this, have the children count the inchworms.

Social Studies:

1. **Salad and Soup Party**

   The children can plan and participate in a salad and soup party for their parents. The groceries will need to be purchased, cleaned, and prepared.

2. **Plant Hunt**

   Go on a hunt to discover how many non-flowering plants such as algae, fungi, lichens, mosses, and ferns are found in the school yard. Make a display. How are these plants different from garden plants?

Group Time (games, language):

1. **Huckle Buckle Bean Stalk**

   A small object such as a plastic flower or acorn may be used for hiding. All the players cover their eyes, except the one who hides the object. After it is hidden, the players stand up and begin to look for it. When one locates it, he doesn't let others know the placement. Instead he quietly takes a seat saying "Huckle Buckle Bean Stalk." The game continues until all players have located the object. The first child

to find the object usually hides it the next time. This game is appropriate for older children.

2. **The Big Turnip—Creative Dramatics**

   First tell the story of *The Big Turnip*. Then pass out an identifying piece of clothing for each character. Hats work well for people and collars or signs for the animals. Retell the story, letting the children act the story out. Use as many characters as you have children. This would be a good outdoors activity.

Cooking:

1. **Vegetable Soup**

   Begin with consomme or soup base. Add whatever vegetables, beans, etc., children want to add and can help to prepare. Make soup a day ahead so that all of the vegetables will be cooked thoroughly.

2. **Indian—Cucumbers and Tomatoes with Yogurt**

   2 medium cucumbers
   2 green onions with tops, chopped
   1 teaspoon salt
   2 tomatoes chopped
   1/2 clove garlic, finely chopped
   2 tablespoons snipped parsley
   1/2 teaspoon ground cumin
   1/8 teaspoon pepper
   1 cup unflavored yogurt

   Cut cucumbers lengthwise into halves. Scoop out seeds. Chop cucumbers. Mix cucumbers, green onions, and salt. Let stand 10 minutes. Add tomatoes. Mix remaining ingredients except yogurt. Toss with cucumber mixture. Cover and refrigerate at least 1 hour. Drain thoroughly. Just before serving, fold in yogurt. Makes 6 servings.

   Source: *Betty Crocker's International Cookbook*. (1980). New York: Random House.

3. **Lettuce or Spinach Roll-ups**

   On clean lettuce or spinach leaves, spread softened cream cheese or cottage cheese. If desired, sprinkle with grated carrots or chopped nuts. Roll them up. Chill and serve.

4. **Carrot Cookies**

1/2 cup honey
1 egg
1/2 cup margarine
1 cup whole wheat flour
1 1/4 teaspoons baking powder
1/4 teaspoon salt

1/2 cup rolled oats
1/2 cup wheat germ
1/2 cup grated raw carrots
1/2 cup raisins
1/2 cup nuts (optional)
1 teaspoon vanilla

Mix all ingredients in a bowl. Drop mixture by spoonfuls onto a lightly greased cookie sheet. Flatten each ball slightly. Bake in a 350-degree oven for approximately 12 minutes.

Multimedia:

The following resources can be found in educational catalogs:

1. Palmer, Hap. *Walter the Waltzing Worm* [record].

2. Raffi. "Oats and Beans and Barley Grow" and "Over in the Meadow" on *Baby Beluga* [record].

3. Seeger, Pete. "Jimmy Crack Corn" on *American Folk Songs* [record].

Books:

The following books can be used to complement the theme:

1. Titherington, Jeanne. (1990). *Pumpkin Pumpkin*. New York: Morrow.

2. Ehlert, Lois. (1990). *Growing Vegetable Soup*. San Diego: Harcourt Brace Jovanovich.

3. Buria, Maria E. (1989). *Billy the Bean*. Downey, CA: Colorful Learnings.

4. Krementz, Jill. (1991). *A Very Young Gardener*. New York: Dial Books for Young Readers.

5. McCann, Sean. (1989). *Growing Things*. Chester Springs, PA: Dufour Editions, Inc.

6. Sanchez, Isidro, & Peris, Carme. (1991). *The Garden*. Hauppauge, NY: Barron's Educational Series, Inc.

7. Stagg, Mildred A., & Lamb, Cecile. (1992). *Song of the Seed*. Cincinnati, OH: Standard Publishing Co.

8. Wilner, Isabel. (1991). *A Garden Alphabet*. New York: Dutton Children's Books.

9. Cooke, Tom (Illus.). (1991). *Bert's Little Garden: A Sesame Street Book*. New York: Random House Books for Young Readers.

10. Florian, D. (1991). *Vegetable Garden*. San Diego: Harcourt Brace Jovanovich.

11. Gerstein, Mordicai. (1993). *Maggie's Garden*. New York: Harper Collins Children's Books.

12. McKissack, Patricia, & McKissack, Frederick. (1991). *Messy Bessy's Garden*. Chicago: Children's Press.

13. Slote, Elizabeth. (1991). *Nelly's Garden*. New York: William Morrow and Co.

14. Christini, Ermanno, & Puricelli, Luigi. (1991). *In My Garden*. Saxonville, MA: Picture Book Studios.

15. Kemp, Moira. (1992). *Round & Round the Garden*. New York: Dutton.

16. Ryder, Joanne. (1992). *The Snail's Spell*. New York: Viking.

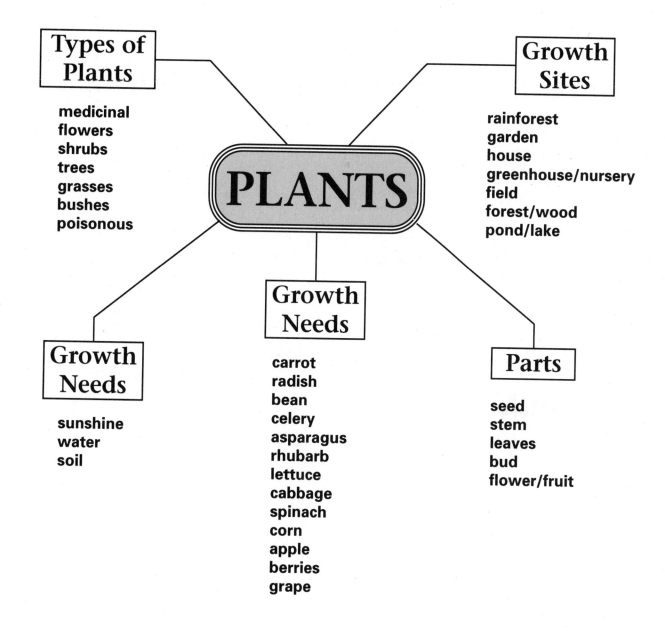

Types of Plants

medicinal
flowers
shrubs
trees
grasses
bushes
poisonous

Growth Sites

rainforest
garden
house
greenhouse/nursery
field
forest/wood
pond/lake

PLANTS

Growth Needs

carrot
radish
bean
celery
asparagus
rhubarb
lettuce
cabbage
spinach
corn
apple
berries
grape

Growth Needs

sunshine
water
soil

Parts

seed
stem
leaves
bud
flower/fruit

Theme Goals:

Through participating in the experiences provided by this theme, the children may learn:

1. Types of plants.

2. Growth of plants.

3. The parts of a plant.

4. Plant growth sites.

5. Plants that provide food.

Concepts for the Children to Learn:

1. Plants are living things that grow.

2. There are many kinds of plants.

3. Some plants grow from seeds.

4. Some plants grow from another plant.

5. Plants need water, sunlight, and soil to grow.

6. People and animals eat some types of plants.

7. The parts of a plant are the stem, roots, leaves, flower/fruit, and seeds.

8. There are different sizes, colors, and shapes of seeds.

Vocabulary:

1. **plant**—living thing, usually green, that grows and changes.

2. **stem**—part of the plant that supports the leaves and grows upward.

3. **leaf**—part of the plant that grows on the stem.

4. **root**—part of the plant that grows into the soil.

5. **seed**—part of plant that can grow into another plant.

6. **vegetable**—a plant grown for food.

7. **fruit**—edible plant product that has seeds.

8. **flower**—a colored plant part that contains seeds.

9. **garden**—ground for growing plants.

10. **sprout**—first sign of growth.

Bulletin Board

The purpose of this bulletin board is to foster numeral recognition. To prepare the bulletin board, construct flowerpots out of construction paper. Color each pot and draw dots on it as illustrated. Hang the pots on the bulletin board. Next, construct the same number of flowers with stems as pots. In the center of each flower, write a numeral. The children can place each flower in the flowerpot with the corresponding number of dots.

Parent Letter

Dear Parents,

Plants will be the focus of our next unit. Through the unit the children will become aware of the parts of a plant as well as discover where plants can be grown and what plants can be eaten.

At School

Some of the learning experiences planned related to plants include:

- listening to the story, *The Plant Sitter*, by Gene Zion.
- sprouting alfalfa seeds to add to a salad.
- walking around our play yard to collect plants.
- playing hopscotch in the shape of a flower.

At Home

There are many ways to foster the concepts of this unit at home. If you have plants, let your child help water them. If you are planning to start a garden, section off a small portion for your child to grow plants.

At mealtimes, identify various parts of plants that are eaten. For example, we eat the leaves of lettuce, the stems of celery, the root of a carrot, and so on.

Plant some flower seeds with your child!

Which flower do you like best?

Music:

1. **"The Seed Cycle"**
   (Sing to the tune of "The Farmer in the Dell")

   The farmer sows his seeds.
   The farmer sows his seeds.
   Hi-ho the dairy-o
   The farmer sows his seeds.

   Other verses:
   The wind begins to blow…
   The rain begins to fall…
   The sun begins to shine…
   The seeds begin to grow…
   The plants grow big and tall…
   The farmer cuts his corn…
   He puts it in his barns…
   And now the harvest is in…

   Children can dramatize the parts for each
   verse.

2. **"This is the Way We Rake the Garden"**
   (Sing to the tune of: "Here We Go Round the
   Mulberry Bush")

   This is the way we rake the garden,
   Rake the garden, rake the garden.
   This is the way we rake the garden,
   So early in the morning.

   Other verses:
   This is the way we plant the seeds…
   This is the way the rain comes down…
   This is the way we hoe the weeds…
   This is the way the garden grows…
   This is the way we pick the vegetables…
   This is the way we eat the vegetables…

3. **"The Farmer in the Dell"** (traditional)

Fingerplays:

MY GARDEN

   This is my garden.
      (extend one hand forward, palm up)
   I'll rake it with care
      (make raking motion on palm with other
      hand)
   And then some flower seeds
      (make planting motion with thumb and
      index fingers)
   I'll plant in there.
   The sun will shine
      (make circle above head)
   And the rain will fall
      (let fingers flutter down to lap)
   And my garden will blossom
      (cup hands together, extend upward slowly
      until fingers stand straight)
   And grow straight and tall.

PLANTS

   Plants need care to help them grow
      (make fist with hand)
   Just like boys and girls you know.
   Good soil, water, sunshine bright.
   Then watch them pop overnight.
      (extend fingers from fist)

Science:

1. Watch Seeds Grow

Two identical plastic transparent plates and blotting paper are needed for this activity. Moisten the blotting paper. Then lay the wet paper on one of the plates. On the top of the paper plate place various seeds—corn, peas, squash, bean, etc. Place the other plate over the seeds to serve as a cover. Tie the plates together tightly. Stand the plate on its edge in a pan containing a half-inch of water. Watch the seeds sprout and grow.

2. Colored Celery

In clear containers place several celery stalks with leaves. In each container add 3 inches of water and drop a different color of food coloring. The leaves of the celery should turn colors in a few hours. Try splitting a celery stalk in half, but do not split the stalk all the way up to the top. Put one half of the stalk in red water, and the other half in blue water. Watch what happens to the leaves.

3. Sunlight Experiment

Place seeds in two jars with a half-inch of soil. Place one jar in a dark place such as a closet or cupboard and avoid watering it. Keep the other jar in a sunny area and water it frequently. Which one grew? Why?

4. Growing Bean Plants

Each child can grow a bean plant.

5. Tasting Plants

Various fruits and vegetables grown from plants should be provided for the children to taste and smell.

6. Feely Box

In the feely box, place different parts of a plant such as root, stem, leaves, flowers, fruit, and buds. The children can feel and verbally identify the part of the plant before looking at it.

7. Root a Vegetable

Place a potato or carrot in a jar, root end down so that one-third is covered by water. A potato can be held upright by inserting toothpicks or nails at three points. This can be rested on the rim of the jar. The children can water as needed. Roots should grow out from the bottom and shoots from the top. Then plant the root in soil for an attractive plant.

8. Beans

Soak dry navy beans in a jar of water overnight. The next day compare soaked beans with dry beans. Note the difference in texture and color. Open some bean seeds that were soaked. A tiny plant should be inside the seed. These can be placed under a microscope for closer observation.

9. Budding Branches

Place a branch that has buds ready to bloom in a jar of water on the science table. Let the children observe the buds bloom. Notice that after all the stored food of the plant is used the plant will die.

Dramatic Play:

1. Greenhouse

Provide materials for a greenhouse. Include window space, pots, soil, water, watering cans, seeds, plants, posters, work aprons, garden gloves, a terrarium, and seed packages to mount on sticks.

2. Jack and the Beanstalk

Act out the story, *Jack and the Beanstalk*. The children can dramatize a beanstalk growing.

3. Vegetable-Fruit Stand

Display plastic fruits and vegetables. Set up a shopping area with carts, cash registers, and play money. Provide a balance scale for children to weigh the produce.

4. **Garden Planting**

   Plant a small garden outdoors. Provide seeds, watering cans, garden tools, gloves, and garden hats.

Arts and Crafts:

1. **Grass Hair**

   Save 1/2-pint milk cartons. The children can decorate the outside of the carton like a face. Place soil in the cartons and add grass seeds. After approximately 7 days the grass will start to grow, and it will look like hair. If the grass becomes too long, have the child give it a haircut.

2. **Flower Collage**

   Collect flowers and weeds. Press the flowers and weeds between paper and books. Old telephone directories can be used. Dry them for 7 to 10 days. The children can use the pressed foliage to create their own collages on paper plates or construction paper.

3. **Seed Pictures**

   Supply the children with paper, paste or glue, and various kinds of seeds. Included may be grass, beans, and unpopped popcorn kernels. The children can express their own creativity through self-created designs.

4. **Nature Tree**

   Cut a branch off a tree and place in a pail of plaster of paris. The children can decorate the tree with a ribbon and different forms of plant life that they have collected or made. Included may be flowers, plants, fruits, vegetables, and seeds.

5. **Leaf Rubbings**

   Place a thin piece of paper over a leaf. Rub gently with the long side of a crayon.

6. **Easel Ideas**

   Cut easel paper into different shapes such as:

- leaves
- flowers
- flowerpots
- fruits and vegetables

7. **Egg Carton Flowers**

   Use egg cartons and pipe cleaners to make flowers. To make the flower stand up, place a pipe cleaner into the egg carton as well as a styrofoam block.

8. **Muffin Liner Flowers**

   Use paper muffin tin liners to make flowers.

9. **Hand and Foot Flowers**

   Create a flower by using the child's hands and feet. Trace and cut two left and right hands and one set of left and right feet. Put one set of hands together to form the top of the flower and the other set (facing down) to form the bottom side. Add a circle to the middle. Cut a stem from green paper and add the green feet, as leaves. This makes a cute Mother's Day idea. Mount on white paper.

Math:

1. **Charting Growth**

   The children can observe the growth of a small plant by keeping a chart of its growth. Record the date of the observation and the height. For convenience, place the chart near the plant table.

2. **Flowerpot Match Game**

   Construct flowerpots. The number constructed will depend upon the developmental appropriateness. Write a numeral on each, beginning with the numeral one. Then make the same number of flowers, varying from one petal to the total number of flowerpots constructed. The children match the flowerpot to the flower with the same number of petals.

3. **Counting and Classifying Seeds**

   Place a variety of seeds on a table. Encourage the children to count and classify them into groups. To assist in counting and classifying, an egg carton with each section given a number from 1 to 12 may be helpful. Encourage the children to observe the numeral and place a corresponding number of seeds in each section.

4. **Plant Growth Seriation**

Construct pictures of plants through stages of growth. Begin with a seed, followed by the seed sprouting. The third picture should be the stem erupting from the soil surface. Next a stem with leaves can be constructed. Finally, flowers can be added to the last picture. This could also be made into a bulletin board.

5. **Seed Match**

Collect a variety of seeds such as corn, pumpkin, orange, apple, lima bean, watermelon, pea, and peach. Cut several rectangles out of white tagboard. On the top half of each rectangle, glue one of the seed types you have collected. Encourage the children to sort the seeds, matching them to those seeds glued on the individual cards.

Social Studies:

1. **Plant Walk**

Walk around the neighborhood and try to identify as many plants as you can.

2. **Play Yard Plants**

Make a map of the play yard. The children can collect a part of each plant located in the playground. The plant samples can be mounted on the map.

3. **Planting Trees**

Plant a tree on your playground. Discuss the care needed for trees.

4. **Family Tree**

Make a Family Tree by mounting a bunch of branches in a pail of dirt. Each child can bring

in a family picture to be placed on a leaf shape and hung on the tree branches.

Large Muscle:

1. **Leaf Jumping**

Cut out eight large leaves from tagboard. Arrange the leaves in a pattern on the floor. Encourage the children to jump from one leaf to another. This game could also be played outdoors by drawing the leaves on the sidewalk with chalk.

2. **Flower Hopscotch**

Design a hopscotch in the form of a flower. Use chalk on a sidewalk outdoors or masking tape can be used indoors to make the form.

3. **Vegetable, Vegetable, Plant**

Play "Vegetable, Vegetable, Plant" as a variation of "Duck, Duck, Goose."

4. **Raking and Hoeing**

Provide the children with hoes and rakes to tend to the play yard.

Field Trips:

1. **Greenhouse**

Visit a greenhouse or a tree nursery to observe the different plants and trees and inquire about their care.

2. **Farm**

Plan a visit to a farm. While there, observe the various forms of plant life.

3. **Florist**

Visit a florist. Observe the different colors, types, and sizes of flowering plants.

Group Time (games, language):

Feltboard Fun

Construct felt pieces representing the stages of a flower's growth. Include a bulb, seed, cuttings, root, stem, leaves, and a flower. During group time, review the name and purpose of each part with the children. The children can take turns coming up to the flannel board and adding the pieces. After group time, the felt pieces should be left out so that the child can reconstruct the growth during self-selected activity period.

Cooking:

1. **Vegetable-Tasting Party**

   Prepare raw vegetables for a tasting party. Discuss the color, texture, and flavor of each vegetable.

2. **Sprouts**

   Provide each interested child with a small jar. Fill the bottom with alfalfa seeds. Fill the jar with warm water and cover with cheesecloth and a rubberband. Each day rinse and fill the jar with fresh warm water. In three or four days the seeds will sprout. The sprouts may be used on sandwiches or salads at lunchtime.

3. **Latkes (Potato Pancakes)**

   2 potatoes, peeled and grated
   1 egg, slightly beaten
   1/4 cup flour
   1 teaspoon salt
   cooking oil

   Mix the ingredients in a bowl. Drop the mixture by tablespoons into hot oil in an electric skillet. Brown on both sides. Drain on paper towels.

4. **Ground Nut Soup (Nigeria)**

   1 large tomato
   1 large potato
   1 onion
   2 cups water
   1 beef boullion cube
   1 cup shelled, unsalted roasted peanuts
   1/2 cup milk
   2 tablespoons rice

   Peel potato and onion. Dice potato, tomato, and onion. Place in saucepan with the water and boullion cube. Boil, covered, for 30 minutes. Chop and add the peanuts, milk, and rice to the boiling mixture. Stir. Lower heat and simmer 30 minutes. Serves 6 to 8.

Multimedia:

The following resources can be found in educational catalogs:

1. "Oats, Peas, Beans and Barley Grow," *Let's Sing Along with Mother Goose* [record]. Farmingdale, NY: Record Guild of America.

2. *Great Bedtime Stories: Jack and the Beanstalk* [record]. New York: A.A. Records Inc.

3. "The Little Nut Tree," [record]. Walt Disney Productions.

Books:

The following books can be used to complement the theme:

1. Fife, Dale H. (1991). *The Empty Lot*. Boston: Little Brown.

2. Politi, Leo. (1993). *Three Stalks of Corn*. New York: Macmillan.

3. Cherry, Lynne. (1990). *The Great Kapok Tree*. San Diego: Harcourt Brace Jovanovich.

4. Bunting, Eve. (1993). *Someday a Tree*. New York: Clarion.

5. Allard, Harry. (1993). *The Cactus Flower Bakery*. New York: Harper Collins.

6. Gibbons, Gail. (1991). *From Seed to Plant*. New York: Holiday House, Inc.

7. Heller, Ruth. (1992). *Plants That Never Ever Bloom*. New York: Putnam Publishing Group.

8. Riehecky, Janet. (1990). *What Plants Give Us: The Gift of Life*. Mankato, MN: Child's World, Inc.

9. Wexler, Jerome. (1991). *Flowers Fruits and Seeds*. New York: Simon and Schuster Trade.

10. Blos, Joan W. (1992). *A Seed, a Flower, a Minute, an Hour*. New York: Simon and Schuster Trade.

11. Taylor, Barbara. (1991). *Growing Plants*. New York: Franklin Watts Inc.

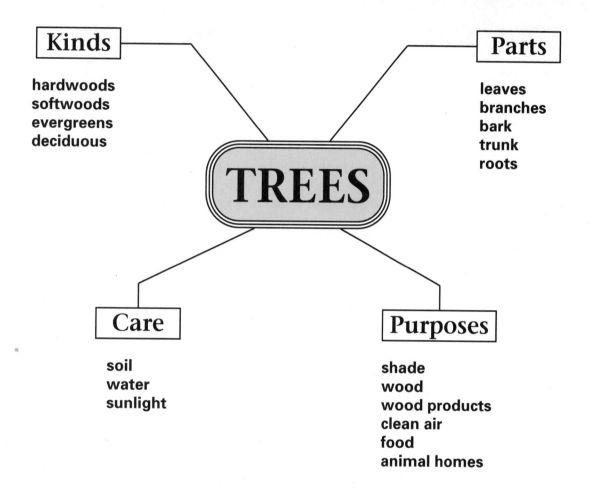

Kinds

hardwoods
softwoods
evergreens
deciduous

TREES

Parts

leaves
branches
bark
trunk
roots

Care

soil
water
sunlight

Purposes

shade
wood
wood products
clean air
food
animal homes

Theme Goals:

Through participating in the experiences provided by this theme, the children may learn:

1. Parts of a tree.

2. Kinds of trees.

3. Care of trees.

4. How trees help us.

Concepts for the Children to Learn:

1. A tree is a large plant.

2. There are many kinds of trees including hardwoods and softwoods.

3. A tree has many parts: leaves, branches, bark, trunk, and roots.

4. The leaves of some trees are like needles.

5. The trunk is the stem of the tree and is covered with bark.

6. The roots of a tree are underground.

7. Roots help the tree stand; they also get water and nutrients from the soil.

8. Sap is a liquid that supplies food to the tree.

9. Trees need soil, water, and sunlight to grow.

10. Trees provide us with wood.

11. Many items are made from wood, such as houses, chairs, tables, some toys, doors, fences, paper, and paper products.

12. Some fruit grows on trees.

13. Apples, bananas, and oranges are examples of fruits that grow on trees.

14. Trees provide homes for many animals.

15. Trees provide us with shade to keep us cool and protect us from the sun.

Vocabulary:

1. **tree**—a large plant.

2. **trunk**—the main stem and largest part of a tree.

3. **bark**—the tough, outer covering of a tree.

4. **sap**—the fluid part of a tree.

5. **root**—the underground part of a plant.

Bulletin Board

The purpose of this bulletin board is to provide numeral identification as well as matching sets of objects to numerals. To prepare the bulletin board construct tree trunks out of brown tagboard. Print a numeral on each trunk. Next, construct treetops out of green tagboard. Draw sets of leaves on each treetop. Trace and cut out treetop shadows from black construction paper. Using the illustration as a guide, attach the shadows and tree trunks to the bulletin board. Adhesive magnet pieces or map tacks can be used by the children to match each tree trunk to the corresponding treetop.

Parent Letter

Dear Parents,

Did you ever stop to think about what our world would be like without trees? Trees serve many purposes; consequently, we will be exploring a theme on trees beginning this week. Through the experiences provided the children will become aware of the parts of a tree, kinds of trees, and, of course, the importance of trees.

At School

We will use wood to build houses, schools, chairs, tables, and all kinds of other objects. We will make paper. We will talk about foods that grow on trees. The foods served at snack time will be those foods that are grown on trees. Some of the week's activities will include:

- creating leaf and bark rubbings in the art area.
- going on a "tree walk" and recording the number and kinds of trees we see.
- cooking with foods we get from trees.
- creating our own books in the writing center.
- planting citrus fruit seeds and an avocado seed.

At Home

Walk around your home and find all the things that are made from wood. Which room contains the most wood items?

Polish your furniture with your child. Show them how to care for fine wood products.

Try preparing the following recipe with your child:

Apple Bake

Core an apple and place it in a dish with a tablespoon or two of water. Sprinkle with cinnamon and a dash of sugar, if desired. Cover and bake at 350 degrees for 20 minutes. If you prefer microwaving, cover with plastic wrap and cook on "high" for five minutes.

Enjoy your child!

Children enjoy a brush as a tool to apply paint.

Music:

1. **"Little Leaves"**
   (Sing to the tune of "Ten Little Indians")

   One little, two little, three little leaves.
   Four little, five little, six little leaves.
   Seven little, eight little, nine little leaves.
   Ten little leaves fall down.

2. **"Foods That Grow on Trees"**
   (Sing to the tune of "The Farmer in the Dell")

   Foods that grow on trees.
   Foods that grow on trees.
   Let's sing a song about
   Foods that grow on trees.

   Apples grow on trees.
   Apples grow on trees.
   Pick them, red and sweet.
   Apples grow on trees.

   Bananas grow on trees.
   Bananas grow on trees.
   Pick them, yellow and long.
   Bananas grow on trees.

   Oranges grow on trees.
   Oranges grow on trees.

   Pick them, sweet and juicy
   Oranges grow on trees.

   Walnuts grow on trees.
   Walnuts grow on trees.
   Pick them, brown and crunchy.
   Walnuts grow on trees.

Fingerplays:

THE APPLE TREE

Way up high in the apple tree
   (raise arms over head)
Two little apples smiled at me.
   (make fists or circles with hands)
I shook that tree as hard as I could
   (move hands as if shaking something)
Down came the apples
   (falling motion with fists)
Mmmmmmmmmmmmmmmmm—were they good!
   (rub tummy)

ORANGE TREE

This is the orange tree with leaves so green
   (raise arms over head, making a circle)
Here are the oranges that hang in between.
   (make fists)

When the wind blows the oranges will fall.
Here is the basket to gather them all.
   (make circle with arms in front of body)

I AM A TALL TREE

I am a tall tree.
I reach toward the sky
   (reach upward with both hands)
Where the bright stars twinkle
And white clouds float by.
   (sway arms above head)
My branches toss high
As the wild winds blow.
   (wave arms rapidly)
Now they bend forward
Loaded with snow.
   (arms out front swaying)
I like it best
When I rock birds to sleep in their nest.
   (place hands at the side of head and close eyes)

THE WIND

Who has seen the wind?
Neither you nor I;
But where the leaves hang trembling,
   (hold hands downward and wiggle fingers)
The wind is passing through.

Who has seen the wind?
Neither you nor I;
But when the trees bow down their heads,
   (move head downward)
The wind is passing by.

Science:

1. **Weighing Nuts**

   Provide a balance scale and acorns, pinecones, or nuts at the science table.

2. **Planting Seeds**

   Collect and plant seeds from fruits that grow on trees such as apples and citrus fruits. Make and record predictions about when the plants will sprout.

3. **Grow An Avocado Tree**

   Remove a seed from an avocado. Peel off the brown outer covering of the seed. Poke three toothpicks into the avocado seed at equal distances from one another. Place the seeds in a glass of lukewarm water with the largest end submerged. Replace the water once a week. Sprouts will appear in about three weeks. When the stem and roots are several inches long, transplant the avocado into a pot that is about 1 inch wider than the avocado.

4. **Leaf Book**

   Collect leaves from various trees. Mount each leaf on a piece of construction paper or tag-board. Then print the name of the tree the leaf represents. Gather the pages and bind with loose-leaf rings. Place the book in the science area for the children to review.

5. **Shade Versus Sun**

   Place an outdoor thermometer in direct sunlight and another beneath the shade of a tree. Compare results. A chart could also be made for this activity and results could be compared for several days.

6. **Pinecone Bird Feeders**

   Collect pinecones. Attach a piece of yarn or string to the stem. Use a plastic knife to spread peanut butter over the pinecone; then roll in birdseed. Hang the bird feeder outside.

7. **Make Paper**

   Cut a piece of screen 7 inches x 11 inches and frame with wood. Tear construction paper or tissues into one-inch pieces. Place the shredded paper pieces in a blender. Add enough water to cover and blend the paper into pulp. Pour the pulp into a 9-inch x 13-inch tray. Use the framed screen to pan the pulp, moving it to get an even layer of pulp. Lift the screen out of the pan in a straight, upward direction. Place the screen on a stack of newspapers. Roll with a rolling pin to squeeze out water. Lift off the newspaper and gently peel the homemade paper from the screen; allow it to dry on paper towels or newspaper.

Dramatic Play:

1. Construction Site

Design a construction site in the dramatic play area. Provide props such as hard hats, blueprints, floor plans, rulers, tape measures, lumber scraps, wooden blocks, and cardboard boxes.

2. Birds

Trace and cut bird masks and wings out of tagboard for the children to wear. Display pictures of trees and birds. Play a tape of bird songs. A variation would be to decorate a climber with green crepe paper to resemble a tree.

Arts and Crafts:

1. Tree Rubbing

Use crayons or chalk to create rubbings of various tree parts. Place leaves under a single sheet of newsprint. Rub the crayon over the top of the paper until the imprint of the leaf appears. Try making additional rubbings using bark and maple seeds.

2. Twig Painting

Twigs from trees can be used as painting tools. Provide the children with trays of tempera paint of a thick consistency and construction paper to create designs. The children may also enjoy experimenting with the twig as a writing tool.

3. Pine Needle Brushes

Cut branches from a pine needle tree. Place the branches at the easel so that the children can use them as brushes to apply paint.

4. Decorating Pinecones

Collect pinecones of different sizes. Place them on the art table with trays of thick colored tempera paints, glitter, glue, yarn, sequins, and strips of paper for the children to decorate the pinecones.

5. Sawdust Playdough

Combine two cups of sawdust, three cups of flour, and one cup of salt. Add water as needed to make a pliable dough. (Sawdust can be obtained, usually at no cost, from a local lumber company.)

6. Textured Paint

Add sawdust to prepared paints for use at the art table or easel.

7. Paper Product Sculptures

Collect magazines, newspapers, boxes, and paper towel rolls for the children to use to create designs and sculptures. Place all of the items on the art table along with glue, scissors, and paint.

8. Make a Tree

Collect paper towel and toilet paper rolls. The children can paint or cover them with construction paper to resemble tree trunks. Branches and leaves can be fabricated from pipe cleaners and construction paper. The branches and leaves can then be attached to the trunk.

Sensory:

1. Wood Shavings

Obtain wood shavings from a local lumber company. Place them in the sensory table along with scoops and pails.

2. Pinecones

Collect pinecones of various sizes and place them in the sensory table. Small boxes, pails, and scoops can be added.

3. Acorns

Collect acorns and allow them to dry thoroughly before placing in the sensory table. Add accessories to encourage participation such as pails, small paper bags, scoops, and spoons.

Large Muscle:

1. Wooden Climber

If available, set up a wooden climber on the playground or in the classroom for the children to practice their climbing skills.

2. Wooden Balance Beam

If available, set up a wooden balance beam in an open area of the classroom. Suggest ways for the children to cross the beam: walking heel to toe, walking sideways, crawling, and walking holding an object. Older children may be able to walk backward.

Field Trips/Resource People:

The following sources can be contacted for more information:

- area forest industries such as paper mills and logging companies.
- Department of National Resources.
- university or county extension offices.
- national, state, and local parks.
- nature centers.
- university departments of biology, botany, construction, and forestry.

Math:

1. Trace Walk

Record the number of trees observed on a walk. If appropriate, the trees might also be classified as "broadleaf" or "evergreen" or by the type of tree, such as maple, oak, pine, etc.

2. Sorting and Counting Activities

The following items can be collected and used for various sorting and counting activities:

acorns
small pinecones
walnuts
pecans
almonds
apple seeds
citrus fruit seeds

3. Items Made From Trees

Collect items from around the classroom for children to sort and classify as those made from trees as "wooden items" and "non-wooden items." Label and provide boxes or similar containers for the children to place the items. If appropriate, the children can count the number of items in each category and record the results.

Social Studies:

1. Family Tree

Cut a tree trunk out of brown tagboard. Cut a treetop out of green tagboard. Attach the trunk and treetop to a bulletin board and display on a wall. Ask the children to bring family photographs that can be displayed on the tree.

Group Time (language, games):

1. Tree Chart

On a large piece of tagboard, print the title, "Things Made from Trees." During group time, present the chart and record the children's responses. Display the completed chart and refer to it throughout the theme.

2. Movement Activity—"Happy Leaves"

Cut leaves out of various colors of construction paper. During group time give each child one leaf. When the children hear the color of their leaf in the following rhyme, they may stand up and move like leaves:

Little red leaves are glad today,
For the wind is blowing them off and away,
They are flying here, they are flying there.
Oh, little red leaves, you are everywhere.

Repeat the rhyme and insert additional color words.

Cooking:

1. **Guacamole Dip**

   1 medium avocado
   2 tablespoons of chopped onion
   1/4 teaspoon chili powder
   1/4 teaspoon garlic salt
   2 tablespoons mayonnaise or salad dressing

   Peel and cut the avocado into pieces and process at medium speed in a blender. Add remaining ingredients and blend. Serve the dip with tortilla or corn chips.

2. **Orange Pecan Cookies**

   1 cup sugar
   3/4 cup softened butter or margarine
   1/4 cup milk
   1 teaspoon vanilla
   1 egg
   2 cups flour
   1/2 cup finely chopped pecans
   2 tablespoons grated orange peel

   1 teaspoon baking powder
   3/4 teaspoon salt

   Combine sugar, butter, milk, vanilla, and egg in a large mixing bowl. Add remaining ingredients and blend well. Drop by rounded teaspoonfuls onto ungreased cookie sheets. Bake for 9–12 minutes or until lightly browned in a 370-degree oven. Remove cookies from sheet and cool.

3. **Prepare any recipes that include:**

almonds	coconuts	nutmeg
apples	dates	olives
apricots	figs	oranges
avocados	grapefruit	peaches
cashews	lemons	pears
cherries	limes	pecans
cinnamon	mangoes	prunes
cloves	maple syrup	walnuts
	nectarines	

   Beware of the potential of children choking on nuts. Avoid using them or grind them finely in recipes for young children.

Books:

The following books can be used to complement this theme:

1. Arnotsky, Jim. (1992). *Crinkleroot's Guide to Knowing the Trees*. New York: Macmillan Children's Book Group.

2. Barker, Cicely M. (1991). *Flower Fairies of the Trees*. New York: Warne, Frederick and Co.

3. Braithwaite, Althea. (1988). *Tree*. Chicago: Dearborn Financial Publishing.

4. Brenner, Barbara, & Garelick, May. (1992). *The Tremendous Tree Book*. Honesdale, PA: Boyds Mill Press.

5. Florian, Douglas. (1990). *Discovering Trees*. New York: Macmillian Children's Book Group.

6. Fowler, Allan. (1990). *It Could Still Be a Tree*. Chicago: Children's Press.

7. Lyon, George-Ella. (1989). *A B Cedar: An Alphabet of Trees*. New York: Orchard Books.

8. National Wildlife Federation Staff. (1991). *Trees are Terrific*. Vienna, VA: National Wildlife Federation.

9. Nelson, JoAnne. (1990). *A Home In a Tree*. New York: McClanahan Books Co.

10. Ryder, Joanne. (1991). *Hello,Tree!* New York: Dutton Children's Books.

11. Thornhill, Jan. (1992). *A Tree In a Forest*. New York: Simon and Schuster Trade.

12. Bunting, Eve. (1993). *Someday a Tree*. New York: Clarion.

13. Ehlert, Lois. (1991). *Red Leaf, Yellow Leaf*. San Diego: Harcourt Brace Jovanovich.

14. Ikeda, Daisaku. (1992). *The Cherry Tree*. New York: Alfred A. Knopf Books for Young Readers.

15. Martin, Bill, Jr., & Archambault, Jan. (1989). *Chicka Chicka Boom Boom*. New York: Simon and Schuster Trade.

16. Sato, Saatoru. (1989). *I Wish I Had a Big, Big Tree*. New York: Lothrop, Lee, & Shepard Books.

17. Behn, Harry. (1992). *Trees*. New York: Henry Holt and Co.

18. Arnold, Caroline. (1990). *A Walk in the Woods*. Eden Praire, MN: Silver Press.

19. Pearce, Q. L., & Pearce, W. L. (1990). *In the Forest*. Eden Praire, MN: Silver Press.

20. Greene, Carol. (1989). *I Can Be a Forest Ranger*. Chicago: Children's Press.

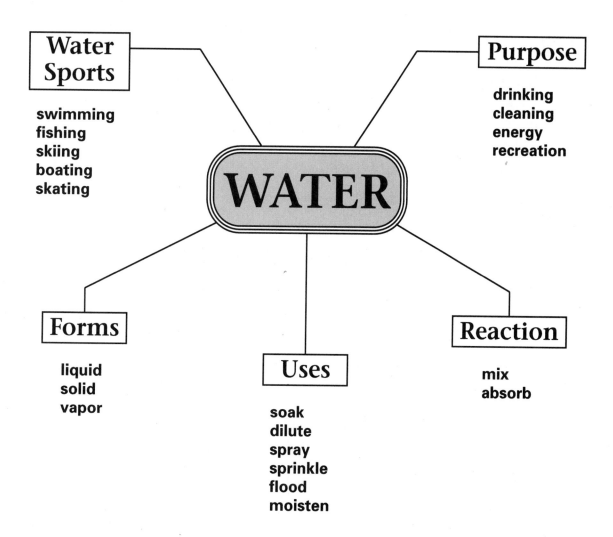

Water Sports

swimming
fishing
skiing
boating
skating

Purpose

drinking
cleaning
energy
recreation

WATER

Forms

liquid
solid
vapor

Uses

soak
dilute
spray
sprinkle
flood
moisten

Reaction

mix
absorb

Theme Goals:

Through participating in the experiences provided by this theme, the children may learn:

1. Uses of water.

2. Forms of water.

3. Water sports.

4. Purposes of water.

Concepts for the Children to Learn:

1. All living things need water.

2. Water takes three forms: liquid, vapor, and solid.

3. Ice is a solid form of water.

4. Steam is a vapor form of water.

5. Some things mix with water; others do not.

6. Some things absorb water; others do not.

7. Some things float when placed on water.

8. Some animals and plants live in bodies of water.

9. Water can be used to soak, dilute, spray, sprinkle, flood, and moisten.

Vocabulary:

1. **water**—a clear, colorless, odorless, tasteless liquid.

2. **lake**—a large body of water surrounded by land.

3. **ocean**—body of salt water.

4. **swimming**—moving yourself through water with body movements.

5. **cloud**—water droplets formed in the sky.

6. **rain**—water that falls from clouds.

7. **snow**—water that freezes and falls from the sky.

8. **liquid**—substance that can be poured.

9. **freeze**—hardened liquid.

10. **melt**—to change from a solid to a liquid.

11. **ice**—water that has frozen.

12. **sink**—to drop to the bottom of a liquid.

13. **float**—to rest on top of a liquid.

Bulletin Board

The purpose of this bulletin board is to develop visual discrimination and matching skills. Construct and color four or five pictures of swimming and water-related items from tagboard. Laminate. Trace these pictures on black construction paper to make shadows. Staple the shadows on the bulletin board. Encourage the children to hang the colored picture over the correct shadow.

Parent Letter

Dear Parents,

Did you know all living things have something in common? All living things need water to survive. Water will be the subject that we will explore with our next unit. The children will become familiar with the forms, uses, and bodies of water, as well as sports that require water to be played.

At School

Some of the learning experiences planned to include water concepts are:

- placing celery stalks in colored water to observe plants' use of water.
- experimenting with objects that sink or float when placed in water.
- washing doll clothes in the sensory table.
- observing ice with magnifying glasses and watching it change from a solid to a liquid.

At Home

There are many ways that you can reinforce water concepts at home. Try any of the following with your child.

- Allow your child to assist in washing dishes after a meal. This will give your child a sense of responsibility and will develop self-esteem.
- Provide water and large paintbrushes for your child to paint sidewalks and fences outdoors.
- Bubbles made with an eggbeater in a container of soapy water are fun for children of all ages!

Enjoy your child!

A water table can be used for science activities.

Music:

"Raindrops"
(Sing to the tune of "London Bridges")

Raindrops falling from the sky,
From the sky, from the sky.
Raindrops falling from the sky
On my umbrella.

Fingerplays:

FIVE LITTLE DUCKS

Five little ducks
    (hold up five fingers)
Swimming in the lake.
    (make swimming motions)
The first duck said,
    (hold up one finger)
"Watch the waves I make."
    (make waves motions)
The second duck said,
    (hold up two fingers)
"Swimming is such fun."
    (smile)
The third duck said,
    (hold up three fingers)

"I'd rather sit in the sun."
    (turn face to sun)
The fourth duck said,
    (hold up four fingers)
"Let's swim away."
    (swimming motions)
The fifth duck said,
    (hold up five fingers)
"Oh, let's stay."
Then along came a motorboat.
With a Pop! Pop! Pop!
    (clap three times)
And five little ducks
Swam away from the spot.
    (put five fingers behind back)

SWIMMING

I can dive.
    (make diving motion with hands)
I can swim.
    (swimming motion)
I can float.
    (hands outstretched with head back)
I can fetch.
But dog paddle
    (paddle like dog)
Is the stroke I do best.

FIVE LITTLE FISHES

Five little fishes swimming in a pond.
    (wiggle five fingers)

The first one said, "I'm tired," as he yawned.
  (yawn)
The second one said, "Well, let's take a nap."
  (put hands together on side of face)
The third one said, "Put on your sleeping cap."
  (pretend to pull on hat)
The fourth one said, "Wake up! Don't sleep."
  (shake finger)
The fifth one said, "Let's swim where it's deep."
  (point down and say with a low voice)
So, the five little fishes swam away.
  (wiggle fingers and put behind back)
But they came back the very next day.
  (wiggle fingers out front again)

THE RAIN

I sit before the window now
  (sit down)
And look out at the rain.
  (shade eyes and look around)
It means no play outside today,
  (shake head)
So inside I remain.
  (rest chin on fist; look sad)

I watch the water dribble down
  (look up and down)
As it turns the brown grass green.
And after a while I start to smile
At nature's washing machine.
  (smile and lean back)

Science:

1. **Painting Sidewalks**

   On a sunny day, allow children to paint sidewalks with water. To do this, provide various paintbrushes and buckets of water. Call attention to the water evaporation.

2. **Measuring Rainfall**

   During spring, place a bucket outside with a plastic ruler set vertically by securing to the bottom. Check the height of the water after each rainfall. With older children, make a chart to record rainfalls.

3. **Testing Volume**

   Containers that hold the same amounts of liquid are needed. Try to include containers that are tall, skinny, short, and flat. Ask the children, "Do they hold the same amount?" Encourage them to experiment by pouring liquids from one container to another.

4. **Freezing Water**

   Freeze a container of water. Periodically, observe the changes. In colder climates, the water can be frozen outdoors. The addition of food coloring may add interest.

5. **Musical Scale**

   Make unique musical tone jars by pouring various levels of water into glass soda bottles. Color each bottle of water differently. Provide the children with spoons, encouraging them to experiment with sounds by tapping each bottle.

6. **Plants Use Water**

   Place celery stalks in colored water. Observe how water is absorbed in its veins.

7. **Chase the Pepper**

   Collect the following materials: water, pepper, shallow pan, piece of soap, sugar. Fill the pan with water and shake the pepper on the water. Then take a piece of wet soap and dip it into the water. What happens? (The pepper moves away from the soapy water to the clear water.) The skin on water pulls and on soapy water the pull is weak. On clear water it is strong and pulls the pepper along. Now take some sugar and shake it into the soapy water. What happens? Sugar gives the skin a stronger pull.

8. **Warm Water/Cold Water**

   Collect the following materials: a small aquarium, a small bottle, food coloring, water. First fill the aquarium with very warm water. Fill the small bottle with colored cold water. Put your thumb on the mouth of the bottle. Hold the bottle sideways and lower it into the warm water. Take away your thumb. What happens? (The cold water will sink to the bottom of the tank. The cold water is heavier than the warm water.) Now fill the tank with cold water and fill the small bottle with colored warm water. What do you predict will happen when you repeat the procedure?

9. **Wave Machine**

Collect the following materials: mineral oil, water, food coloring, transparent jar. Fill the jar 1/2 to 2/3 full with water. Add a few drops of food coloring. Then add mineral oil to completely fill the jar. Secure the lid on the jar. Tilt the jar slowly from side to side to make waves. Notice that the oil and water have separate layers and do not stay mixed after the jar is shaken.

10. **Water and Vinegar Fun**

Collect the following materials: two small jars with lids, water, and white vinegar. Pour water into one jar and an equal amount of vinegar into the other jar. Replace caps. Then let the children explore the jars of liquids and discuss the similarities. Then let the children smell each jar.

Dramatic Play:

1. **Fire Fighter**

Place hoses, hats, coats, and boots in the dramatic play area.

2. **Doll Baths**

Fill the dramatic play sink with water. Children can wash dishes or give dolls baths.

3. **The Beach**

Provide towels, sunglasses, umbrellas, pails, shovels, and beach toys for the children to use indoors or outdoors.

4. **Canoeing**

Bring a canoe into the classroom or onto the play yard. Provide paddles and life vests for the children to wear.

Arts and Crafts:

1. **Liquid Painting**

Paper, straws, thin tempera, and spoons can be placed on the art table. Spoon a small amount of paint onto paper. Using a straw, blow paint on the paper to make a design.

2. **Bubble Prints**

Collect the following materials: 1/2 cup water, 1/2 cup liquid soap, food coloring, straws, and light-colored construction paper. Mix together the water, soap, and food coloring in a container. Place a straw in the solution and blow until the bubbles reach about one to two inches over the top of the container. Remove the straw and place a piece of paper over the jar. The bubbles will pop as they touch the paper, leaving a print.

3. **Wet Chalk Drawings**

Chalk, paper, and water in a shallow pan are needed for this activity. The children can dip chalk into water and then draw on paper. Encourage children to note the difference between wet and dry chalk.

Sensory:

1. **Colored Ice**

Fill the sensory table with colored ice cubes for the children to explore.

2. **Sink and Float**

Fill sensory table with water. Provide the children with a variety of items that will sink and float. Let them experiment. A chart may be prepared listing items that sink and float.

3. **Boating**

Fill the water table. Let the children add blue food coloring. Provide a variety of boats for them to play with.

4. Moving Water

Provide the children with a variety of materials that move water. Include the following:

- sponges
- basters
- eye droppers
- squeeze bottles
- funnels
- measuring cups
- pitchers
- empty film canisters
- plastic tubing

Large Muscle:

Catch Me

Children form a circle with one child in the middle. While walking in a circle they chant:

_____ over the water.
_____ over the sea.
_____ caught a tunafish.
But he can't catch me!

(Insert child's name.)

On "me," all the children stoop quickly. If the child in the middle touches another child, the fish, before he stoops, that child is it. Likewise, he now goes into the middle. This game is for older children.

Math:

Measuring

Assorted measuring cups in a variety of sizes can be added to the sensory table or sandbox.

Group Time (games, language):

Water Fun

Discuss the various recreational uses of water. Included may be swimming, boating, ice fishing, ice skating, fishing, and canoeing. Encourage the children to name their favorite water activities. Prepare a chart using each child's name and favorite water activity along with a small picture of that activity. Display in the room.

Cooking:

1. Fruit Ice

Mix 1/2 can partially thawed juice concentrate with 2 cups of crushed ice in the blender. Liquify until the contents become snowy. Serve immediately.

2. Floating Cake—Philippines

2 cups sweet rice flour
1 cup water
1/2 to 3/4 cup sugar
1/2 cup toasted sesame seeds, hulled
1 cup grated coconut

Mix rice flour and water. Form into 10 to 20 small balls. Flatten each ball into a round or elongated shape and drop into 8 to 10 cups boiling water. As each cake floats to the surface, remove from water with a slotted spoon. Roll in grated coconut and coat with sugar and sesame seeds. Adult supervision is required. Makes 4 servings.

WATER PLAY AND SENSORY EXPERIENCES

Sensory experiences are especially appealing to young children. They delight in feeling, listening, smelling, tasting, and seeing. They also love to manipulate objects by pulling, placing, pouring, tipping, shoving, as well as dipping. As they interact, they learn new concepts and solutions to old problems. When accompanied by other children, these experiences lead to cooperative, social interactions. As a result, the child's egocentricity is reduced, allowing him to become less self-centered.

Containers

Begin planning sensory experiences by choosing an appropriate container. Remember that it should be large enough so that several children may participate at any given time. If you select a dishpan, due to its size, you may want to use several. Other containers that may be used include a commercially made sensory/water table, baby bathtub, wash tub, pail, wading pool, sink, or bath tub.

Things to Add to Water

A variety of substances can be added to water to make it more inviting. Food coloring is one example. Start by individually choosing and adding one primary color. Later soaps can be added. These may be in liquid or flake form. Baking soda, cornstarch, and salt will affect the feel of the water. Baby and vegetable oil may leave a residue on the child's hand. Extracts add another dimension. Lemon, almond, pine oil, peppermint, anise, and orange all permit a variety for the child. On the other hand, ice cubes allow the child to experience an extreme touch.

Tools and Utensils

A wide variety of household tools can be used in the water play table. Measuring cups, small pitchers, small pots and pans, and film canisters can all be used for pouring. Scoops, spoons, turkey basters, small squeeze bottles, and funnels can be used for transferring the liquid from one container to another. Pipes, rubber hoses, sponges, wire whips, and eggbeaters all can be used for observing water in motion. Plastic toys, corks, spools, strainers, boots, etc., also encourage exploration.

Other Sensory Experiences

There are wide varieties of other materials that can be used in the sensory table. Natural materials such as sand, gravel, rocks, grain, mud, wood chips, clay, corn, and birdseed can be used. Children also enjoy having minnows and worms in the table. They delight in visually tracking the minnow and worm movement. As they attempt to pick them up, eye-hand coordination skills are practiced. Styrofoam pieces and shavings are attractive materials that can lend variety.

A strange mixture called goop is a fun material to play with. To prepare goop, empty 1 box of cornstarch into a dishpan or similar container. Sprinkle a few drops of food coloring on the cornstarch. Add small amounts of water (about 1/2 cup) at a time and mix with a spoon or with fingers. (This is a unique sensory experience!) The mixture feels hard when you touch it on the surface, yet melts in your hands when you pick some up! (This will keep for up to one week if kept covered when not in use. You will probably need to add water the next time you use it.)

Silly putty is just as easy to prepare as goop. This mixture is prepared by combining 1 part of liquid starch, 2 parts of white glue, and dry tempera paint for color. Begin by measuring the liquid starch first, as it will prevent the glue from sticking to the measuring cup. Mix with a spoon, adding single tablespoons of liquid starch to get the right consistency. Then knead with hands. Store in an airtight container (such as a zip-lock bag) in the refrigerator. You will be thrilled to find that it will keep for several weeks.

Enjoy yourself with the children, but always change the sensory experiences on a daily basis. In doing so, you stimulate the child's curiosity as well as

provide a meaningful curriculum.

For health purposes, children should be encouraged to wash their hands after sensory play.

Multimedia:

The following resources can be found in educational catalogs:

Jenkins, Ella. *Rhythms of Childhood with Ella Jenkins* [record]. Folkway Records.

Books:

The following books can be used to complement the theme:

1. Raffi. (1987). *Down by the Bay*. New York: Crown Publishers, Inc.

2. Blocksma, Mary. (1987). *Rub-a-Dub-Dub-What's in the Tub?* Chicago: Children's Press.

3. Crespo, George. (1993). *How the Sea Began*. New York: Clarion Books.

4. Arnosky, Jim. (1990). *Deer at the Brook*. New York: Morrow.

5. Brown, Marc. (1991). *All Wet*. Boston: Little, Brown.

6. Day, Alexandra. (1992). *River Parade*. New York: Puffin.

7. Gantschev, Ivan. (1991). *The Moon Lake*. Saxonville, MA: Picture Book Studios.

8. Hoban, Julia. (1993). *Amy Loves the Rain*. New York: Harper Collins.

9. Jones, Rebecca C. (1991). *Down at the Bottom of the Deep Dark Sea*. New York: Macmillan.

10. McDowell, Josh, & McDowell, Dottie. (1988). *Katie's Adventure at Blueberry Pond*. Elgin, IL: David Cook.

11. Koch, Michelle. (1993). *World Water Watch*. New York: Greenwillow.

12. Cristini, Ermanno, & Puricelli, Luigi. (1991). *In the Pond*. Saxonville, VA: Picture Book Studio, Ltd.

13. Fowler, Allan. (1992). *It Could Still Be Water*. Chicago: Children's Press.

14. Peters, Lisa. (1991). *Water's Way*. New York: Arcade Publishing, Inc.

15. Russell, Naomi. (1991). *The Stream*. New York: Dutton Children's Books.

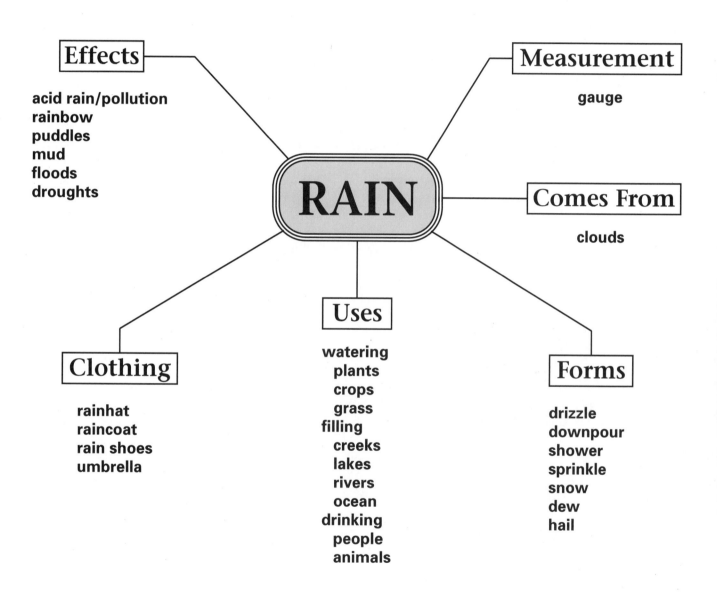

Effects

acid rain/pollution
rainbow
puddles
mud
floods
droughts

Measurement

gauge

RAIN

Comes From

clouds

Clothing

rainhat
raincoat
rain shoes
umbrella

Uses

watering
  plants
  crops
  grass
filling
  creeks
  lakes
  rivers
  ocean
drinking
  people
  animals

Forms

drizzle
downpour
shower
sprinkle
snow
dew
hail

Theme Goals:

Through participating in the experiences provided by this theme, the children may learn:

1. Uses of rain.

2. Effects of rain.

3. Clothing worn for protection from the rain.

4. Forms of rain.

5. Origin of rain.

6. The tool used for the measurement of rain.

Concepts for the Children to Learn:

1. Rain falls as a liquid from the clouds.

2. Rain can fall in the form of drizzle, hail, snow, or a shower.

3. Rain can be used for watering lawns and filling lakes.

4. A rainbow sometimes appears when it rains while the sun is shining.

5. A rainbow is colorful.

6. An umbrella is used in the rain to keep us dry.

7. Raincoats, hats, and rubber shoes are rain clothing.

8. Puddles can form during a rainfall.

9. The amount of rain can be measured in a water gauge.

10. Farmers need rain to water the crops.

Vocabulary:

1. **rain**—water that falls from the clouds.

2. **rainbow**—a colorful arc formed when the sun shines while it is raining.

3. **puddle**—rain collection on the ground.

4. **umbrella**—a shade for protection against rain.

5. **snow**—frozen rain.

6. **gauge**—a tool for measuring rain.

Bulletin Board

The purpose of this bulletin board is to develop an awareness of sets, as well as to identify written numerals. Construct clouds out of gray tagboard. Write a numeral on each cloud. Cut out and laminate. Next, trace and cut cloud shadows from construction paper. Attach the shadows to the bulletin board. A set of raindrops, from one to 10, should be attached underneath each cloud shadow. Magnet pieces or push pins and holes in the cloud piece can be used for the children to match each cloud to a corresponding shadow, using the raindrops as a clue.

Parent Letter

Dear Parents,

"Rain, rain, go away. Come again some other day," is a familiar nursery rhyme. It is one that we may often hear as a unit on rain begins. Through the experiences provided, the children will become aware of the uses and forms of rain as well as how rainbows are created.

At School

The following activities are just a few that have been planned for the rain unit:

- a visit by TV 8's weatherman. Tom Hector will be coming at 2:00 pm on Tuesday to show us a video made for preschoolers that depicts various weather conditions.
- finding out about evaporation by setting out a shallow pan of water and marking the water level each day.
- creating a rainbow on a sunny day outdoors with a garden hose.

At Home

To develop language skills, practice this rain poem with your child:

> Rain on the green grass
> And rain on trees.
> Rain on the rooftops,
> But not on me!!

Use an empty can or jar to make a rain gauge. Place the container outdoors to measure rainfall. Several gauges could be placed in various places in your yard.

Enjoy your child!

Rain serves many purposes.

Music:

"Rainy"
(Sing to the tune of "Bingo")

There was a day when we got wet
and rainy was the weather
R-A-I-N-Y R-A-I-N-Y R-A-I-N-Y
and rainy was the weather.

Repeat each verse eliminating a letter and
substituting it with a clap until the last chorus
is all claps to the same beat.

Fingerplays:

LITTLE RAINDROP

This is the sun, high up in the sky.
   (hold hands in circle above head)
A dark cloud suddenly comes sailing by.
   (slide hands to side)
These are the raindrops.
   (make raining motion with fingers)
Pitter patter down.
Watering the flowers,
   (pouring motion)
Growing on the ground.
   (hands pat the ground)

RAINY DAY FUN

Slip on your rain coat.
   (pretend to put coat on)
Pull up your galoshes.
   (pull up galoshes)
Wade in puddles,
Make splishes and sploshes.
   (make stomping motions)

THUNDERSTORM

Boom, bang, boom, bang!
   (clap hands)
Rumpety, lumpety, bump!
   (stomp feet)
Zoom, zam, zoom, zam!
   (swish hands together)
Rustles and bustles
   (pat thighs)
And swishes and zings!
   (pat thighs)
What wonderful noises
A thunderstorm brings.

RAIN

From big black clouds
   (hold up arms)
The raindrop fell.
   (pull finger down in air)

Drip, drip, drip one day,
   (hit one finger on palm of hand)
Until the bright sunlight changed them
Into a rainbow gay!
   (make a rainbow with hands)

Source of first four fingerplays: Wilmes, Dick & Liz. *Everyday Circle Times.* Building Block Publications.

THE RAIN

I sit before the window now
   (seat yourself, if possible)
And I look out at the rain.
   (shade your eyes and look around)
It means no play outside today
   (shake head, shrug)
So inside I remain.
   (rest chin on fist, look sorrowful)
I watch the water dribble down
   (follow up-to-down movements with eyes)
And turn the brown grass green.
   (sit up, take notice)
And after a while I start to smile
At Nature's washing machine.
   (smile, lean back, relax)

Source: Cromwell, Hibner, & Faitel. *Finger Frolics—Finger Plays for Young Children.*

Science:

1. **Tasting Water**

   Collect tap water, soda water, mineral water, and distilled water. Pour the different types of water into paper cups and let children taste them. Discuss the differences.

2. **Evaporation**

   The children can pour water into a jar. Mark a line at the water level. Place the jar on a window ledge and check it every day. The disappearance is called evaporation.

3. **Catching Water**

   If it rains one day during your unit, place a bucket outside to catch the rain. Return the bucket to your science table. Place a bucket of tap water next to the rainwater and compare.

4. **Color Mixing**

   Using water and food coloring or tempera, mix the primary colors. Discuss the colors of the rainbow.

Dramatic Play:

1. **Rainy Day Clothing**

   Umbrellas, rain coats, hats, rain shoes, and a tape containing rain sounds should be added to the dramatic play area. Use caution when selecting umbrellas for this activity. Some open quickly and can be dangerous.

2. **Weather Station**

   A map, pointer, adult clothing, and pretend microphone should be placed in the dramatic play area. The children can play weather person. Pictures depicting different weather conditions can be included.

Arts and Crafts:

1. **Eyedropper Painting**

   Use eyedroppers filled with colored water as applicators.

2. **Waxed Paper Rainbows**

   Cut waxed paper in the shape of large rainbows. Then prepare red, yellow, green, and blue crayon shavings. After this, the children can sprinkle the crayon shavings on one sheet of waxed paper. Place another sheet of waxed paper on the top of the sheet with sprinkled crayon. Finally, the teacher should place a linen towel over the top of the waxed paper sheets. A warm iron should be applied to melt the two pieces together. Cool and attach a string. Hang from the window. (This activity needs constant adult supervision.)

3. **Rainbow Yarn Collage**

   Using rainbow-shaped paper and rainbow-colored yarn, the children can make rainbow yarn collages.

4. Thunder Painting

Tape record a rain or thunderstorm. Leave this tape with a tape recorder and earphones at the easel. Grey, black, and white paint can be provided. Let the children listen to the rainstorm and paint to it. Ask the children how the music makes them feel.

5. Rainbow Mobiles

Pre-cut rainbow arcs. On these, the children can paste styrofoam packing pieces. After this, they can paint the pieces. Display the mobiles in the room.

Sensory:

Add to the sensory table:

- water with scoops, cups, and spoons.
- sand and water (make puddles in the sand).
- rainbow-colored sand, rice, and pasta.
- rainwater

Large Muscle:

Worm Wiggle

The purpose of this game is to imitate worm motions. Show the children how to lie on their stomachs, holding their arms in at their sides. The children should try to move forward without using their hands or elbows like a worm would wiggle.

Field Trips/Resource People:

1. Reflection

Take a walk after it rains. Enjoy the puddles, overflowing gutters, and swirls of water caught by sewers. Look in the puddles. Does anyone see a reflection? Look up in the sky. Do you see any clouds, the sun, or a rainbow? What colors are in a rainbow?

2. The Weather Person

Take a field trip to a television station and see what equipment a weather person uses.

Math:

Rainbow Match

Fabrics of all the colors of the rainbow can be cut into pieces. The children can sort these and group them into different colors, textures, and sizes.

Group Time (games, language):

1. Creative Thinking

Read this poem to your children and then ask them, "Why didn't I get wet?" You may have to read the poem again or you may have to encourage the children to use their imagination since the answer is not in the poem.

RAIN

Rain on green grass
and rain on the tree.
Rain on the rooftop,
But not on me!

Source: Wilmes, Liz & Dick. *Everyday Circle Times*. Illinois: Building Block Publications.

2. Jump in Puddles

This game is played like "Musical Chairs." The puddles are made from circles on the floor with one child in each and one less circle than children so one child is out of the circles. On the signal, "Jump in the puddles," the children have to switch puddles. The child who was out has a chance to get in a puddle. The child who does not get into a puddle waits until the next round. This can be played indoors or outdoors. Hula hoops could also be used in small groups of four children using three hoops. (This activity is most appropriate for older children.)

Miscellaneous:

1. **Cut and Tell Story: "The Rainbow's End"**

   Source: Warren, Jean. *Cut and Tell Scissor Stories for Spring*. Everett, WA: Totline Press, Warren Publishing House.

2. **Flannelboard Stories**

   Source: Stangl, Jean. *Flannel Graphs—Flannel Board Fun for Little Ones*. Belmont, CA: David S. Lake Publishers.

Cooking:

Rainbow Fruits

Serve a different colored snack each day. An example would be to correspond with the colors of the rainbow.

- strawberries
- oranges
- lemon finger gelatin (see a gelatin box for recipe)
- blueberries added to yogurt
- grape juice
- grapes or blackberries
- lettuce salad

Multimedia:

The following resources can be found in educational catalogs:

1. *Color Me a Rainbow* [record]. Melody House Records.

2. *Follow the Clouds* [record]. Melody House Records.

3. *Raindrops* [record]. Melody House Records.

4. *Adventures in Sound* [record]. Melody House Records.

Books:

The following books can be used to complement the theme:

1. Szilagyi, Mary. (1985). *Thunderstorm*. New York: Bradbury.

2. Gay, Marie-Louise. (1989). *Rainy Day Magic*. Morton Grove, IL: Albert Whitman.

3. Stevenson, James. (1988). *We Hate Rain!* New York: Greenwillow.

4. Stolz, Mary. (1990). *Storm in the Night*. New York: Harper Collins.

5. Wiesner, David. (1990). *Hurricane*. New York: Clarion Books.

6. O'Neill, Mary. (1989). *Hailstones and Halibut Bones*. New York: Doubleday.

7. Markle, Sandra. (1993). *A Rainy Day*. New York: Orchard Books.

8. Kachenmeister, Cheryl. (1989). *On Monday When it Rains*. Boston: Houghton Mifflin.

9. Koch, Michele. (1993). *World Water Watch*. New York: Greenwillow.

10. Martin, Bill, Jr., & Archambault, John. (1988). *Listen to the Rain*. New York: Henry Holt.

11. Polacco, Patricia. (1990). *Thunder Cake*. New York: Putnam.

12. Moncure, Jane B. (1990). *Rain: A Great Day for Ducks*. Mankato, MN: Child's World, Inc.

13. Wyler, Rose. (1989). *Raindrops and Rainbows*. New York: Simon and Schuster Trade.

14. Cole, Sheila. (1991). *When the Rain Stops*. New York: Lothrop, Lee, & Shepard Books.

15. Corrin, Ruth. (1990). *It Always Rains for Jackie*. New York: Oxford University Press.

16. Ehlert, Lois. (1988). *Planting a Rainbow*. San Diego: Harcourt Brace Jovanovich.

17. Hallinan, P. K. (1991). *My Very Best Rainy Day*. Nashville, TN: Ideals Publishing Corp.

18. Serfozo, Mary. (1990). *Rain Talk*. New York: Macmillan Children's Books Group.

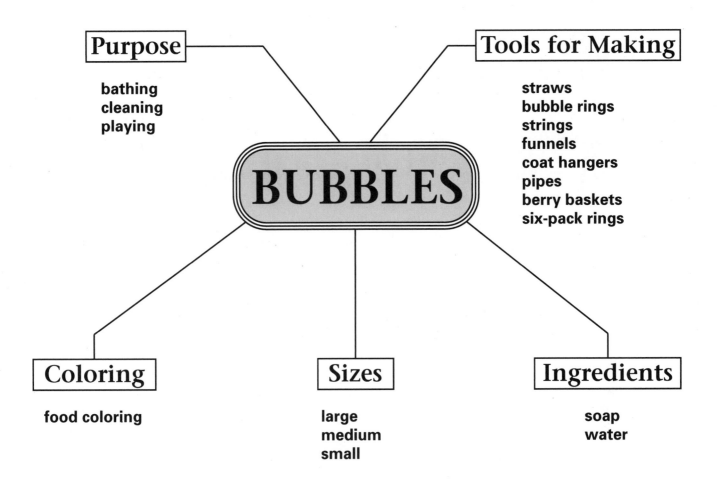

Purpose

bathing
cleaning
playing

Tools for Making

straws
bubble rings
strings
funnels
coat hangers
pipes
berry baskets
six-pack rings

BUBBLES

Coloring

food coloring

Sizes

large
medium
small

Ingredients

soap
water

Theme Goals:

Through participating in the experiences provided by this theme, the children may learn:

1. Purposes of bubbles.

2. Bubble ingredients.

3. Tools for making bubbles.

4. Colors of bubbles.

5. Bubble shapes.

6. Ways to create bubbles.

7. Sizes of bubbles.

Concepts for the Children to Learn:

1. Bubbles are made with soap and water.

2. Bubbles are all around us in foods, baths, water, and drinks.

3. Food coloring can be used to add color to bubbles.

4. Bubbles can be created by blowing or by waving a tool.

5. Bubbles have a skin that holds air inside of them.

6. Straws, bubble rings, strings, funnels, and coat hangers can be used as tools to make bubbles.

Vocabulary:

1. **bubble**—a round circle that has a skin and contains air.

2. **bubble skin**—the outside of the bubble that holds the air.

3. **bubble solution**—a mixture of water and liquid soap.

4. **bubble wand**—a tool used to make bubbles.

Bulletin Board

The purpose of this bulletin board is to promote the active exploration of household items that can be used to make bubbles. Collect items such as pipe cleaners, funnels, spools, six-pack rings, berry baskets, and scissors. Construct and label boxes and/or pockets to hold items on the bulletin board. Containers of bubble solution should be placed near the bulletin board for the children to experiment making bubbles with the household items. Provide towels in the area to encourage the children to assist in wiping up spills.

Parent Letter

Dear Parents:

What do you get when you mix water and soap? Bubbles! The children will make many fascinating discoveries as we focus on a Bubbles theme. Through experiences provided, the children will learn the ingredients used in making bubbles, size of bubbles, and tools for making bubbles.

At School

Some of the learning experiences planned to highlight bubble concepts are:

- Washing dolls and dishes in the sensory table.
- Testing many bubble solution recipes.
- Making bubbles with common household items such as plastic berry baskets, funnels, straws, pipe cleaners, spools, and scissors.
- Creating prints of bubbles in the art area.

At Home

Try the following activities with your child to reinforce bubble concepts at home:

- Allow your child to assist in washing dishes after a meal. This experience will give your child a sense of responsibility and promote self-esteem, as well as heighten his/her awareness of the purpose of bubbles for cleaning.
- Prepare the following bubble solution with your child, then blow some bubbles! You need one cup of water, two tablespoons of liquid dish soap, and one tablespoon of glycerine (optional). Enjoy!

Have a good time with your child!

Catching bubbles outdoors is a good science experience.

Music:

1. **"Pop! Goes the Bubble"**
   (Sing to the tune of "Pop! Goes the Weasel")

   Soap and water can be mixed.
   To make a bubble solution.
   Carefully blow,
   Now, watch it go!
   Pop! Goes the bubble!

2. **"Can you Blow a Big Bubble?"**
   (Sing to the tune of "The Muffin Man")

   Can you blow a big bubble?
   A big bubble, a big bubble?
   Can you blow a big bubble,
   With your bubble gum?

3. **"I'm a Little Bubble"**
   (Sing to the tune of "I'm a Little Teapot")

   I'm a little bubble, shiny and round.
   I gently float down to the ground.
   The wind lifts me up and then I drop.
   Down to the dry ground where I pop.

4. **"Ten Little Bubbles"**
   (Sing to the tune of "Ten Little Indians")

   One little, two little, three little bubbles.
   Four little, five little, six little bubbles.
   Seven little, eight little, nine little bubbles.
   Ten bubbles floating to the ground.

5. **"Here's a Bubble"**
   Here's a bubble, here's a bubble.
   Big and round; big and round.
   See it floating gently,
   See it floating gently,
   To the ground; to the ground.

Fingerplays:

HERE IS A BUBBLE

Here is a bubble
   (make a circle with thumb and index finger)
And here's a bubble
   (make a bigger circle with two thumbs and
   index finger)
And here is a great big bubble I see.
   (make a large circle with arms)

100

Let's count the bubbles we've made.
One, two, three.
   (repeat prior actions)

DRAW A BUBBLE

Draw a bubble, draw a bubble.
Make it very round.
   (make a shape in the air with index finger)
Draw a bubble, draw a bubble.
No corners can be found.
   (repeat actions)

Science:

1. **Bubble Solutions**

    Encourage the children to assist in preparing the following bubble solutions. (Note: The use of glycerine in preparing the bubble solution is optional. It helps to provide a stronger skin on the bubble, but the solutions can be prepared without this ingredient.)

    ### Recipe #1

    1/4 cup liquid dish soap
    1/2 cup water
    1 teaspoon sugar

    ### Recipe #2: Outdoor Use

    3 cups water
    2 cups liquid dish soap (Joy detergent)
    1/2 cup light corn syrup

    ### Recipe #3

    2/3 liquid dish soap
    1 gallon of water
    1 tablespoon glycerine

2. **Bubble Gadgets**

    Prepare a bubble solution and make some bubbles! Try and use of the following to make great bubbles.

    - plastic berry baskets
    - pipe cleaners or thin electrical wire shaped into wands
    - six-pack holders
    - egg poacher trays
    - funnels
    - scissors—hold the blades and dip the finger holders into the bubble solution
    - tin cans—open at both ends
    - paper cups—poke a hole in the bottom of a paper cup. Dip the rim into a bubble solution and blow through the hole.
    - plastic straws—use a single straw or tape several together in a bundle.
    - straws and string—thread three feet of thin thread through two plastic straws. Tie the string together. Hold the straws and pull them to form a rectangle with the string. Dip into a bubble solution and pull upward. As you move the frame, a bubble will form. Bring the two straws together to close off the bubble. This technique requires practice.
    - Hula Hoop—fill a small wading pool with two inches of bubble solution. The Hula Hoop can be used as a giant wand by dipping the hoop in a solution and lifting it up carefully.

3. **Wet/Dry**

    While blowing bubbles with the children, try touching a bubble with a dry finger. Repeat using a wet finger. What happens? You will observe that bubbles break when they touch an object that is dry.

4. **Bubble Jar**

    Fill a small plastic bottle half-full of water. Add a few drops of food coloring, if desired. Add baby oil or mineral oil to completely fill the jar. Secure the bottle tightly. Then slowly tilt the bottle from side to side. When this occurs, the liquid in the jar resembles waves. Bubbles can be created by shaking the bottle. Encourage the children to observe these reactions.

5. **Air Bubbles in Food**

    Examine the air bubbles in pieces of bread, Swiss cheese, and carbonated drinks.

6. **Bubbling Raisins**

    Place two or three raisins in a small bottle of sparkling mineral water. Secure the cap and watch the bubbles form as the raisins sink and float.

Dramatic Play:

1. **Housekeeping**

   Fill the sink in the dramatic play area with soapy water. Provide dishes, dish cloth, towels, and a dish rack for the children to wash the dishes.

2. **Hair Stylist**

   Set up a hair stylist studio in the dramatic play area. Include props such as a cash register, empty shampoo and hair spray containers, mirrors, brushes, combs, barrettes, curlers, discarded hair dryer and curling irons, towels, and smocks. Display pictures of hairstyles and hair products. (Caution: Cut the electric cords off the hair dryers and curling irons to prevent possible injuries.)

Arts and Crafts:

1. **Bubble Prints**

   For each bubble print color desired, mix one part liquid tempera paint with two parts liquid dish soap in a small container. Place a straw in the solution and blow until the bubbles rise above the rim of the container. Remove the straw and place a piece of paper over the bubbles. As the bubbles break, they will leave a print on the paper. (Each child will need a straw for this activity. A pin may be used to poke holes near the top of the straws to prevent the children from accidentally sucking in the paint mixture.)

   Variation: Small bubble wands can be dipped into the paint bubble solution and blown so the bubbles will land on a piece of paper, either at the easel or on the ground outdoors.

2. **Bubble Gum Wrapper Collages**

   Collect wrappers from bubble gum to be placed on the art with paper and glue. The children can use these materials to create collages.

3. **Bubble Paint Containers**

Collect containers that hold commercially prepared bubble solutions. Recycle the containers by using them to hold various colors of paints at the easel or art table.

Sensory:

1. **Wash Dolls**

   Fill the sensory table with warm water and add a few tablespoons of dish soap. Provide plastic dolls, washcloths, and towels.

2. **Dish Washing**

   Place plastic dishes and dishcloths in the sensory table filled with warm soapy water. A dish drying rack could be set up nearby or towels provided to dry the dishes.

3. **Bubble Bath**

   Purchase or make bubble bath soap to put in the sensory table with scoops, measuring cups, and pails.

4. **Bubble Solution**

   The sensory table can be used to hold a bubble solution and bubble-making tools.

5. **Pumps and Water**

   Fill the sensory table with water. Add water pumps, turkey basters, and siphons to create air bubbles in the water.

Field Trips/Resource People:

1. **Hair Stylist**

   Visit a hair stylist to watch a customer receive a shampoo.

2. **Pet Groomer**

   Invite a pet groomer to demonstrate giving a dog a bath.

Math:

1. Bubble Count

If appropriate, encourage the children to blow a set of bubbles that you specify. For example, if you say the number "three," the children would try to blow three bubbles.

2. Bubble Wand Sort

Collect small commercially manufactured bubble wands and place them in a small basket. These wands can be sorted by size or color. They could also be counted or placed in order by size.

3. Geometric Bubble Shapes

Attach the ends of two straws together with duct tape or paper clips, creating the desired shapes. Six straws will be needed to make a pyramid and 12 to make a cube. The frames can be dipped into bubble solutions and observed.

Group Times (games, language):

1. What's Missing?—Game

Place several items to prepare bubbles on a tray. At group time, show and discuss the items. To play the game, cover the tray with a towel and carefully remove one item. Children then identify the missing item. The game can be made more challenging by adding more items to the tray, or by removing more than one item at a time.

2. Bubbles—Creative Dramatics

Guide the children through a creative dramatics activity as they pretend to be bubbles. They can act out being:

- a tiny bubble
- a giant bubble
- a bubble floating on a windy day
- a bubble landing on the grass
- a bubble floating high in the air
- a bubble in a sink
- a bubble in a piece of bread

3. Favorite Bubble Gum Chart

At the top of a piece of tagboard, print the caption "Our Favorite Bubble Gum." Along the left-hand side, glue bubble gum wrappers representing different brands or flavors. Present the chart at group time and ask each child to choose one as his/her favorite. Record the children's names or place their pictures next to the response. If appropriate, count the number of "votes" each brand received and print in on the chart. Display the chart in the classroom and refer to it throughout the unit.

Cooking:

1. Bubbly Beverage

6-oz. can frozen orange juice
6-oz. can frozen lemonade
6-oz. can frozen limeade
6-oz. can frozen pineapple juice (optional)
1 liter lemon-lime soda, chilled
1 liter club soda, chilled

Combine ingredients in a punch or large bowl. Stir to blend the ingredients. Serve over ice, if desired.

2. Root Beer

5 gallons cold water
5 lbs. white sugar
3-oz. bottle root beer extract
5 lbs. dry ice

In a large stone crock or plastic container (do not use metal) mix sugar with 1 gallon of water. Add the remainder of the water and root beer extract. Stir. Carefully add the dry ice. After the ice melts, the root beer can be transferred into other containers to store for 2–3 days.

Books:

The following books can be used to complement this theme:

1. Gaban, Jesus. (1992). *Tub Time for Harry*. Milwaukee, WI: Gareth Stevens.

2. Kudrna, C. Imbior. (1986). *To Bathe a Boa*. Minneapolis, MN: Carolrhoda Books.

3. Noble, Kate. (1992). *Bubble Gum*. Silver Seahorse.

4. Stevens, Kathleen. (1987). *The Beast in the Bathtub*. New York: Harper Collins.

5. Wood, Audrey. (1991). *King Bidgood's in the Bathtub*. San Diego: Harcourt Brace.

6. Mayer, Mercer. (1992). *Bubble Bubble*. Roxbury, CT: Rain Birds Production.

7. Simon, Seymour. (1985). *Soap Bubble Magic*. New York: Lothrop, Lee and Shepard Books.

8. Pluckrose, Henry. (1990). *Clean It!* New York: Franklin Watts, Inc.

9. Winer, Yvonne, & McLean-Carr, Carol Aitkin. (1987). *Never Snap at a Bubble*. Dominguez Hills, CA: Educational Insights.

10. Schubert, Ingrid, & Schubert, Dieter. (1985). *Magic Bubble Trip*. Brooklyn, NY: Kane-Miller.

11. Bridell, Norman. (1992). *Clifford Counts Bubbles*. New York: Scholastic Inc.

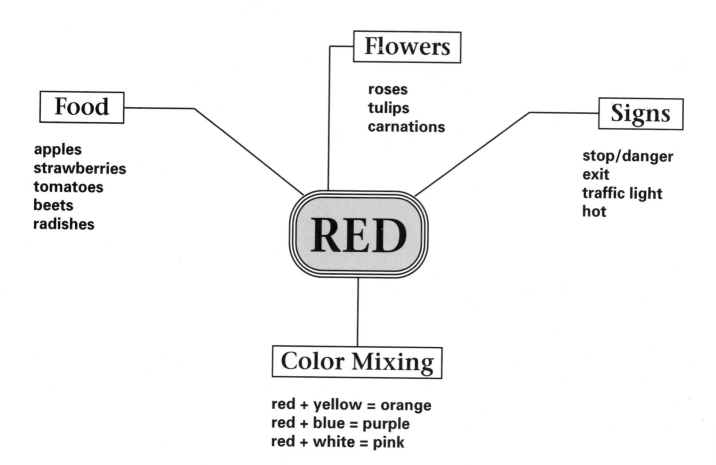

Flowers

roses
tulips
carnations

Food

apples
strawberries
tomatoes
beets
radishes

Signs

stop/danger
exit
traffic light
hot

RED

Color Mixing

red + yellow = orange
red + blue = purple
red + white = pink

Theme Goals:

Through participating in the experiences provided by this theme, the children may learn:

1. Red is a color.

2. Some foods are red.

3. Many objects are red.

4. Red can be mixed with other colors to make different colors.

Concepts for the Children to Learn:

1. Red is a primary color.

2. Some foods, such as tomatoes and strawberries, are red.

3. Red and yellow mixed together make orange.

4. Red and blue mixed together make purple.

5. Red and white mixed together make pink.

6. Some fire trucks and fire hydrants are red.

7. A stop sign is colored red.

8. Some roses, tulips, and carnations are red.

Vocabulary:

1. **red**—a primary color.

2. **primary colors**—red, yellow, and blue.

Bulletin Board

The purpose of this bulletin board is to reinforce the mathematical skills of matching sets of objects to a written numeral. Green produce baskets or other small baskets can be hung on the bulletin board for a strawberry-counting bulletin board. Attach baskets to the bulletin boards using staples or push pins. Collect small plastic strawberries, or make strawberries out of tagboard. On each basket mark a numeral. The children can place the appropriate number of strawberries into each basket.

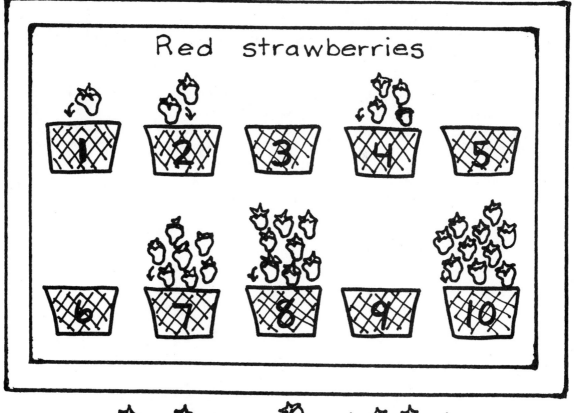

Parent Letter

Dear Parents,

Colors are everywhere and they make our world beautiful. That's why we'll focus on a specific color—red! It's a popular color with young children and many objects in our world are red. The experiences provided will also help the children become aware of colors that are formed when mixed with red.

At School

A few of the curriculum experiences include:

- mixing the color red with yellow and blue to make orange and purple.
- setting up an art store in the dramatic play area where the children can act out the buying and selling of art supplies.
- exploring red-colored crayons, markers, pencils, chalk, paint, and paper.
- filling the sensory table with red goop.

At Home

To reinforce the concepts in this unit, try the following activities at home with your child:

- To develop observation skills look around your house with your child for red items. How many red objects can you find in each room?
- Prepare red foods for meals such as apples, strawberries, tomatoes, and jam.
- Prepare red ice cubes to cool your drinks. To do this, just add a few drops of red food coloring to the water before freezing it.

Enjoy making colorful discoveries with your child.

Sponges and red paint can make interesting designs.

Fingerplays:

TULIPS

Five little tulips–red and bright
   (hold up hand)
Let us water them every day.
   (make sprinkle motion with other hand)
Watch them open in the bright sunlight.
   (cup hand, then open)
Watch them close when it is night.
   (close hand again)

MY APPLE

Look at my apple, it's red and round.
   (make ball shape with hands)
It fell from a tree down to the ground
   (make downward motion)
Come let me share my apple, please do!
   (beckoning motion)

My mother can cut it right in two—
   (make slicing motion)
One half for me and one half for you
   (hold out two hands, sharing halves)

FIVE RED APPLES

Five red apples in a grocery store.
   (hold up five fingers)
Bobby bought one, and then there were four.
   (bend down one finger)
Four red apples on an apple tree.
Susie ate one, and then there were three.
   (bend down one finger)
Three red apples. What did Alice do?
Why, she ate one, and then there were two.
   (bend down one finger)
Two red apples ripening in the sun;
Timmy ate one, and then there was one
   (bend down one finger)
One red apple and now we are done;
I ate the last one, and now there are none.
   (bend down last finger)

Science:

Mixing Colors

Place 2 or 3 ice cube trays and cups filled with red-, yellow-, and blue-colored water on the science table. Using an eyedropper, the children can experiment mixing colors in the ice cube trays. Smocks should be provided to prevent stained clothing.

Dramatic Play:

1. **Art Store**

   Set up an art supply store. Include paints, crayons, markers, paper, chalk, brushes, money, and cash register.

2. **Fire Station**

   Fire fighter hats can be added to the dramatic play area.

3. **Colored Hats**

   After reading *Caps for Sale* by Esphyr Slobodykina, set out colored hats for children to retell the story.

Arts and Crafts:

1. **Red Paint**

   Red and white paint can be provided at the easels. By mixing these colors, children can discover shades of red.

2. **Red Crayons, Markers, etc.**

   Red markers, crayons, and chalk can be placed on a table in the art area. The children can observe the similarities and differences between these various items.

3. **Red Paper**

   Watercolors and red paper can be placed on a table in the art area.

4. **Red Crayon Rubbings**

   Red crayons, red paper, or both can be used to do this activity. Place an object such as a penny, button, or leaf under paper. Use the flat edge of a crayon to color over the item. An image of the object will appear on the paper.

5. **Paint Blots**

   Fold a piece of paper in half. Open up and place a spoon of red paint on the inside of the paper. Refold paper and press flat. Reopen and observe the design. Add two colors such as blue and yellow and repeat process to show color mixing.

6. **Paint Over Design**

   Paint over a crayon picture with watery red paint. Observe how the paint will not cover it.

7. **Glitter Pictures**

   The children make a design using glue on a piece of paper. Then shake red glitter onto glue. Shake the excess glitter into a pan.

8. **Red Fingerpaint**

   Red fingerpaint and foil should be placed on an art table. Yellow and blue paint can be added to explore color mixing.

Sensory:

1. **Red Water**

   Fill the sensory table with water and red food coloring. The children can add coloring and observe the changes.

2. **Red Shaving Cream**

   Shaving cream with red food coloring added can be placed in the sensory table. During self-selected play the children can explore the shaving cream.

3. **Red Goop**

   Mix together red food coloring, 1 cup corn-starch, and 1 cup water in sensory table.

4. **Red Silly Putty**

   Mix together red food coloring, 1 cup liquid starch, and 2 cups white glue. This mixture usually needs to be stirred continuously for an extended period of time before it jells.

Large Muscle:

1. **Ribbon Dance**

   Attach strips of red crepe paper to short wooden dowels or unsharpened pencils to make ribbons. The children can use the ribbons to move to their favorite songs.

2. **Red Bird, Red Bird**

   The children should form a circle by holding hands. Then choose a child to be a bird and start the game. Children chant:

   Red bird, red bird through my window
   Red bird, red bird through my window
   Red bird, red bird through my window
   Oh!

   The bird goes in and out, under the children's arms. The bird stops on the word "Oh" and bows to the child facing him. This child becomes the new bird. The color of the bird can be determined by the color of the clothing of each child picked to be the bird.

Field Trips/Resource People:

1. **Art Store**

   Visit an art store. Observe all the red items for sale.

2. **Take a Walk**

   Take a walk around the neighborhood and look for red objects.

3. **Floral Shop**

   Visit a floral shop and specifically observe red flowers.

4. **Fire Station**

   Visit a fire station. Note the color of the engine, hats, sirens, etc.

5. **Resource People**

   Invite the following resource people to the classroom:

   • artist
   • gardener
   • fire fighter

Math:

1. **Color Cards**

   Construct color cards that start with white and gradually become cherry red. The children can sequence the cards from white to red or red to white. Discontinued sample color cards could be obtained from a paint store.

2. **Bead Stringing**

   Yarn and a variety of colored beads should be available to the children. After initial exploration, the children can make patterns with beads. Example: red, yellow, red, yellow, red.

3. **Colored Bags**

   Place three bags labeled red, yellow, and blue and a variety of blocks on a table. The children can sort the blocks by placing them in the matching colored bag.

Social Studies:

1. **Discussion about Colors**

   During group time discuss colors and how they make us feel. Hold up a color card and ask a child how it makes him feel.

2. **Color Chart**

   Construct a "My Favorite Color Is…" chart. Encourage each child to name his favorite color. After each child's name, print his favorite color with a colored marker. Display the chart in the classroom.

3. **Colored Balloons**

   Each child should be provided with a balloon. The balloons should be the colors of the rainbow: red, orange, yellow, green, blue, and purple. Arrange the children in the formation of a rainbow. Children with red balloons should stand together, etc. Take a picture of the class. Place the picture on the bulletin board.

Group Time (games, language):

1. **Colored Jars**

   Collect five large clear jars. Fill 3 with red water, 1 with yellow water, and 1 with blue water. Show children the 3 red jars. Discuss the color red. Discuss that it can make other colors too. Show them the yellow jar. Add yellow to red. What happens? Add blue water to other red jar. What happens? Discuss color mixing.

2. **Play "Red Light, Green Light"**

   Pick one child to be your traffic light. Place the "traffic light" about 30 feet away from the other children facing away from children who have formed a long line. With back to children, the traffic light says, "green light." Children try to creep toward the traffic light. Traffic light may then say, "red light" and turn toward the children. Children must freeze. The traffic light tries to see if any children are still at the starting line. The game continues with "green light." The first child to reach the traffic light becomes the new light.

Cooking:

1. Raspberry Slush

Thaw and cook 4 packages of 10-ounce frozen raspberries for 10 minutes. Rub the cooked raspberries through strainer with wooden spoon. Cool. Add 1 can (6 ounces) of frozen lemonade concentrate, thawed. Just before serving, stir in 2 quarts of ginger ale, chilled. Makes 24 servings, about 1/2 cup each.

2. Red Pepper Paste—West Africa

1/4 cup dry red cooking wine
1 teaspoon ground red pepper
3/4 teaspoon salt
1/4 teaspoon ground ginger
1/8 teaspoon ground cardamom
1/8 teaspoon ground coriander
1/8 teaspoon ground nutmeg
1/8 teaspoon cloves
1/8 teaspoon ground cinnamon
1/8 teaspoon black pepper
1/8 of a medium onion
1 small clove garlic
1/4 cup paprika

Place all ingredients except paprika in blender container. Cover and blend on high speed until smooth, scraping the sides of the blender frequently. Heat paprika in 1 quart saucepan for 1 minute. Add spice mixture gradually, stirring until smooth. Heat, stirring occasionally, until hot, about 3 minutes. Cool.

3. Pink Dip

Mix 2/3 cup mayonnaise or salad dressing, 2 tablespoons Red Pepper Paste, and 1 tablespoon lemon juice. Serve with celery sticks.

Source: *Betty Crocker's International Cookbook.* (1980). New York: Random House.

Multimedia:

The following resources can be found in educational catalogs:

1. Jenkins, Ella. *I Know the Colors in the Rainbow* [record].

2. *Play & Learn Colors* [IBM software, PK–1]. Remarkable.

Books:

The following books can be used to complement the theme:

1. Graham, Bob. (1987). *The Red Woolen Blanket.* Boston: Little, Brown & Co.

2. Hill, Ari. (1986). *The Red Jacket Mix-Up.* New York: Golden Press.

3. Brown, Margaret Wise. (1989). *Big Red Barn.* New York: Harper & Row.

4. Williams, Vera B. (1988). *Three Days on a River in a Red Canoe.* New York: Morrow.

5. Reiss, John J. (1987). *Colors.* New York: Macmillan.

6. Lundell, Margaretta. (1989). *The Land of Colors.* New York: Putnam.

7. *Baby's Red Picture Book*. (1989). Arburn, ME: Ladybird Books.

8. DeVito, Pam. (1989). *Lydia & the Purple Paint*. Mount Desert, ME: Windswept House.

9. Sklenitzha, Franz S. (1988). *The Red Sports Car*. New York: Barron.

10. Imershein, Betsy. (1989). *Finding Red Finding Yellow*. San Diego: Harcourt Brace Jovanovich.

11. Yardley, Joanna. (1991). *The Red Ball*. San Diego: Harcourt Brace Jovanovich.

12. Rikys, Bodel. (1992). *Red Bear*. New York: Dial Books for Young Readers.

13. Carroll, Kathleen S. (1992). *One Red Rooster*. Boston: Houghton Mifflin Co.

14. Woolfitt, Gabrielle. (1992). *Red*. Minneapolis: Carolrhoda Books, Inc.

15. Broger, Achium. (1991). *Red Armchair*. Wilmington, DE: Atonium Books.

16. Serfozo, Mary. (1988). *Who Said Red?* New York: Macmillan Children's Book Group.

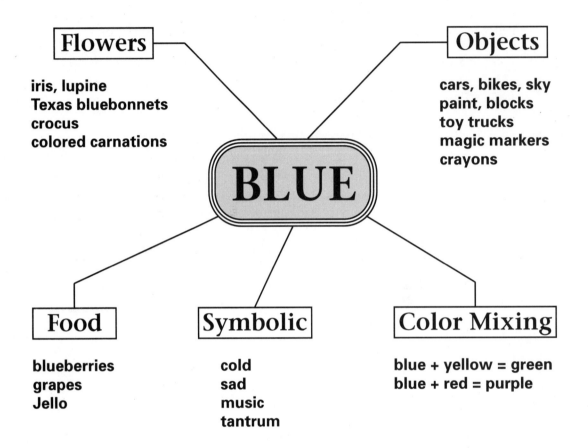

Flowers

iris, lupine
Texas bluebonnets
crocus
colored carnations

Objects

cars, bikes, sky
paint, blocks
toy trucks
magic markers
crayons

BLUE

Food

blueberries
grapes
Jello

Symbolic

cold
sad
music
tantrum

Color Mixing

blue + yellow = green
blue + red = purple

Theme Goals:

Through participating in the experiences provided by this theme, the children may learn:

1. Blue is the color of many objects.

2. A type of berry is colored blue.

3. Some flowers are colored blue.

4. Blue can be mixed with other colors.

Concepts for the Children to Learn:

1. Blue is the name of a color.

2. Mixing blue with yellow makes green.

3. Blue mixed with red makes purple.

4. Some cars and bikes are a blue color.

5. On sunny, clear days the sky is a blue color.

6. Blueberries and grapes are examples of a blue-colored food.

7. There are many shades of blue.

8. An iris can be colored blue.

Vocabulary:

1. **blue**—a primary color.

2. **primary colors**—red, yellow, and blue.

3. **tints**—are created by adding white to a color.

4. **hue**—created by adding black to a color.

Bulletin Board

The purpose of this bulletin board is to develop visual discrimination skills. A blue bulletin board can be constructed by focusing on familiar objects. Draw pictures of many familiar objects on tagboard. Color them various shades of blue. Cut the objects out and laminate. Next, trace the pictures, allowing 1/4-inch borders, on black construction paper. Cut out shadow pieces and hang on the bulletin board. Add a magnet piece to each shadow and picture. The children can match each picture to its corresponding shadow.

Parent Letter

Dear Parents,

Colors! Colors! Colors! We will be now focusing our activities on the color blue. The children will learn that blue can be mixed with red to make purple. Yellow mixed with blue makes green. The children will also become aware that many familiar objects are blue in color. Blue, moreover, represents many different things—sadness, cold, music, etc.

At School

Some of the learning experiences planned for this unit include:

• singing a song called "Two Little Bluejays."
• looking out our blue windows in the classroom.
• playing in a paint store in the dramatic play area.
• fingerpainting with blue paint.
• eating blueberries for snack.

At Home

You can make almost any meal entertaining by occasionally adding a small amount of food coloring to one of your food items. Children often find this amusing. The food coloring adds interest to your food and meal times become fun! Try adding a drop or two to milk, vanilla pudding, mashed potatoes, scrambled eggs, or cottage cheese. Does the color of a food affect its taste? (Try drinking green milk!) You be the judge! To further develop an awareness of color, identify foods that are red, blue, yellow, etc. This improves memory, classification, and expressive language skills.

Have a great time helping your child discover the color blue!

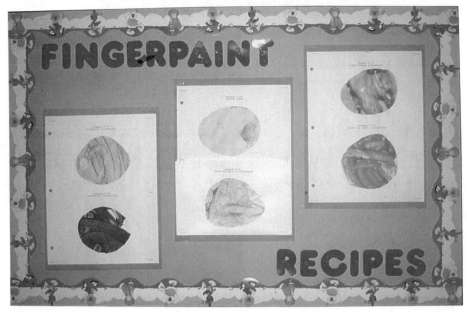

Constructing a bulletin board with items that are blue is one way to learn about colors.

Music:

1. **"Two Little Bluejays"**
   (Sing to the tune of "Two Little Blackbirds")

   Two little bluejays
   sitting on a hill
   One named Sue
   One named Bill.

   Fly away Sue
   Fly away Bill.
   Come back Sue
   Come back Bill.

   Two little bluejays
   sitting on a hill
   One named Sue
   One named Bill.

   To add interest, you can substitute names after the song has been sung several times. The children will enjoy hearing their names.

2. **"Finding Colors"**
   (Sing to the tune of "The Muffin Man")

   Oh, can you find the color blue,
   The color blue, the color blue?
   Oh, can you find the color blue,
   Somewhere in this room?

Science:

1. **Just One Drop**

   Each child will need a smock for this activity. Also, provide a glass of water and blue food coloring. Encourage the children to add a drop of blue food coloring to the water. Watch as the water becomes a light blue. Add a few more drops of food coloring, observing as the blue water turns a darker shade.

2. **Blue Color Paddles**

   Construct blue color paddles out of stiff tagboard and blue overhead transparency sheets. Make a form for the paddle out of tagboard, leaving the inside empty. Put the sheet of blue transparency paper on the back; glue and trim. The children can hold the paddle up to their eyes and see how the colors have changed.

3. **Blue Windows**

   Place blue-colored cellophane or acetate sheets over some of the windows in the classroom. It is fun to look out the windows and see the blue world.

4. Dyeing Carnations

Place the stem of a white carnation in a bottle of water with blue food coloring added on the science table. Observe the change of the petal colors.

Dramatic Play:

Paint Store

Provide paintbrushes, buckets, and paint sample books. The addition of a cash register, play money, and pads of paper will extend the children's play.

Arts and Crafts:

1. Arm Dancing

Provide each child with two blue crayons and a large sheet of paper. Play music encouraging the children to color, using both arms. Because of the structure of this activity, it should be limited to older children.

2. Sponge Painting

Collect sponge pieces, thick blue tempera paint, and sheets of light blue paper. If desired, clothespins can be clipped on the sponges and used as handles. To use as a tool, dip the sponge into blue paint and print on light blue paper.

3. Easel Ideas

- Feature different shades of blue paint at the easel.
- Use blue paint on aluminum foil.
- Add whipped soap flakes to blue paint.
- Add a container of yellow paint to the easel. Allow the children to mix the yellow and blue paints at the easel. This activity can be extended by providing red and blue tempera paint.

4. Fingerpainting

Blue fingerpaint and large sheets of paper should be placed in the art area.

5. Melted Crayon Design

Grate broken blue crayons. Place the shreddings on one square of waxed paper 6 inches x 6 inches. On top of the shreddings, place another 6-inch x 6-inch piece of waxed paper. Cover with a dishtowel or old cloth. Apply heat with a warm iron for about 30 seconds. Let the sheets cool, and the child can trim them with scissors. These melted crayon designs can be used as nice sun catchers on the windows. (This activity needs to be closely supervised. Only the teacher should handle the hot iron.)

Sensory:

Additions to the Sensory Table

1. Water With Blue Food Coloring

2. Blue Goop

Mix together blue food coloring, 1 cup cornstarch, and 1 cup of water.

Large Muscle:

1. Painting

Provide a bucket of blue-colored water and large paintbrushes. Encourage the children to paint the sidewalks, building, fence, sandbox, etc.

2. Blue Ribbon Dance

Make blue streamer ribbons by attaching blue crepe paper to unsharpened pencils. Play lively music and encourage the children to move to the music.

Field Trips:

1. "Blue" Watching

Walk around your center's neighborhood and observe blue items. Things to look for include cars, bikes, birds, houses, flowers, etc. When you return, have the children dictate a list. Record their responses.

2. **Paint Store**

Visit a local paint store. Observe all the different shades of blue paint. Look carefully to see if they look similar. Ask the store manager for discarded sample cards. These cards can be added to the materials to use in the art area.

Social Studies:

Eye Color

Prepare an eye-color chart with the children. Colors on the chart should include blue, brown, and green. Under each category, record the children's names who have that particular eye color. Extend the activity by adding the number of children with each color.

Group Time (games, language):

1. **Bluebird, Bluebird**

The children should join hands and stand in a circle. Construct one bluebird necklace out of yarn and construction paper. Choose one child to be the first bluebird. This bluebird weaves in and out of the children's arms while the remainder of the children chant:

"Bluebird, bluebird through my window
Bluebird, bluebird through my window
Bluebird, bluebird through my window
Who will be the next bluebird?"

At this time the child takes off the necklace and hands it to a child he would like to be the next bluebird.

2. **I Spy**

The teacher says, "I spy something blue that is sitting on the piano bench," or other such statements. The children will look around and try to figure out what the teacher has spied. Older children may enjoy taking turns repeating, "I spy something on the _____."

Cooking:

1. **Blueberries**

Wash and prepare fresh or frozen blueberries for snack. Blueberry muffins are also appropriate for this theme.

2. **Blueberry Muffins**

2 tablespoons sugar
1 3/4 cups flour
2 1/2 teaspoons baking powder
3/4 teaspoon salt
1 egg
1/2 cup milk
1/3 cup salad oil

Mix all of the ingredients together. Add 2 tablespoons of sugar to 1 cup frozen or fresh blueberries. Mix slightly and gently add to the batter. Bake at 400 degrees for approximately 25 minutes.

3. **Cream Cheese and Crackers**

Tint cream cheese blue with food coloring and spread on crackers.

4. **Cupcakes**

Add blue food coloring to a white cake mix. Fill paper cupcake holders with the batter and bake as directed.

- colors of clothing/types of clothing/patterns of fabrics (stripes, polka dots, plaid)
- shoes (boots, shoes with buckles, shoes with ties, shoes with velcro, slip-on shoes, jelly shoes) Also, number of eyelets on shoes, number of buckles
- ages in years
- number of brothers/sisters
- hair/eye color
- birthdays in certain months
- name cards
- first letter of names
- last names
- rhyming names
- animal or word that starts with same sound as your name (Tiger-Tom)
- give each child a turn at something while putting rugs away (blowing a bubble, strumming a guitar, hugging puppet)
- play "I Spy" by saying, "I spy someone wearing blue pants and a Mickey Mouse sweatshirt."
- play a quick game of "Simon Says" and then have Simon tell where the children are to go next.

- "Two Little Blackbirds"
Two little blackbirds sitting on a hill
One named Jack, one named Jill
Fly away Jack, fly away Jill,
Come back Jack, come back Jill.
Two little blackbirds sitting on a hill,
One named Jack, one named Jill.

- "I Have a Very Special Friend"
(Sing to the Tune of "Bingo")
I have a very special friend,
Can you guess his name-o?
J-A-R-E-D, J-A-R-E-D, J-A-R-E-D,
And Jared is his name-o.

- "I'm Looking For Someone"
I'm looking for someone named Kristen,
I'm looking for someone named Kristen,
If there is someone named Kristen here now,
Stand up and take a bow.
(Or, Stand up and go to lunch.)

- "Where, Oh, Where Is My Friend"
Where, oh, where is my friend Travis?
Where, oh, where is my friend Travis?
Where, oh, where is my friend Travis?
Please come to the door.

- "How Did You Come to School Today?"
How did you come to school today,
How did you come on Monday? (Child responds)
He came in a blue car,
Came in a blue car on Monday.

- "One Elephant Went Out to Play"
One elephant went out to play
Upon a spider's web one day.
He had such enormous fun
That he called for another elephant to come.

Group Dismissal

- hop like a bunny
- walk as quiet as a mouse
- tiptoe
- walk backward
- count steps as you walk
- have footsteps for group to walk on or a winding trail to follow

- "This Train" (Tune: "This Train is Bound for Glory")
This train is bound for the lunchroom,
This train is bound for the lunchroom,
This train is bound for the lunchroom,
Katie, get on board.
Matthew, get on board.
Zachary, get on board.
Afton, get on board.
- Change lunchroom to fit situation.

Fillers

- "One Potato"
One potato, two potato, three potato, four
Five potato, six potato, seven potato, more.

- "And One and Two"
And one and two and three and four,
And five and six and seven and eight.
(Repeat faster)

- "Colors Here and There"
Colors here and there,
Colors everywhere.
What's the name of this color here?

- "This is What I Can Do"
This is what I can do,
Everybody do it, too.
This is what I can do,
Now I pass it on to you.

- "A Peanut Sat on a Railroad Track"
A peanut sat on a railroad track,
Its heart was all a-flutter.
Engine Nine came down the track,
Toot! Toot! Peanut butter!

  - apple-applesauce
  - banana-banana split
  - orange-orange juice

- "Lickety Lick"
Lickety lick, lickety lick,
The batter is getting all thickety thick.
What shall we bake?
What shall we bake?
A great, big beautiful carrot cake.

Change "carrot" to any kind of cake

- "I Clap My Hands"
I clap my hands. (Echo)
I stamp my feet. (Echo)
I turn around. (Echo)
And it's really neat. (Echo)
I touch my shoulders. (Echo)
I touch my nose. (Echo)
I touch my knees. (Echo)
And that's how it goes. (Echo)

Multimedia:

The following resources can be found in educational catalogs:

1. *Color Me a Rainbow* [record]. Melody House.

2. *There's Music in the Colors* [record]. Kimbo Records.

3. Palmer, Hap. "Colors" on *Learning Basic Skills Through Music* [record].

4. *Colors* [30-minute video]. Edu-vid.

5. *Pink Pete's ABCs* [Mac software, PK–2]. Orange Cherry.

Books:

The following books can be used to complement this theme:

1. Prelutsky, Jack (1990). *Beneath the Blue Umbrella*. New York: Greenwillow.

2. dePaola, Tomie. (1983). *The Legend of the Bluebonnet: An Old Tale of Texas*. New York: Putnam.

3. Pryor, Ainslie. (1988). *The Baby Blue Cat Who Said No*. New York: Viking.

4. Kaler, Rebecca. (1993). *Blueberry Bear*. Bloomington, IN: Inquiring Voices Press.

5. Dubar, Joyce. (1991). *I Want a Blue Banana*. Boston: Houghton Mifflin.

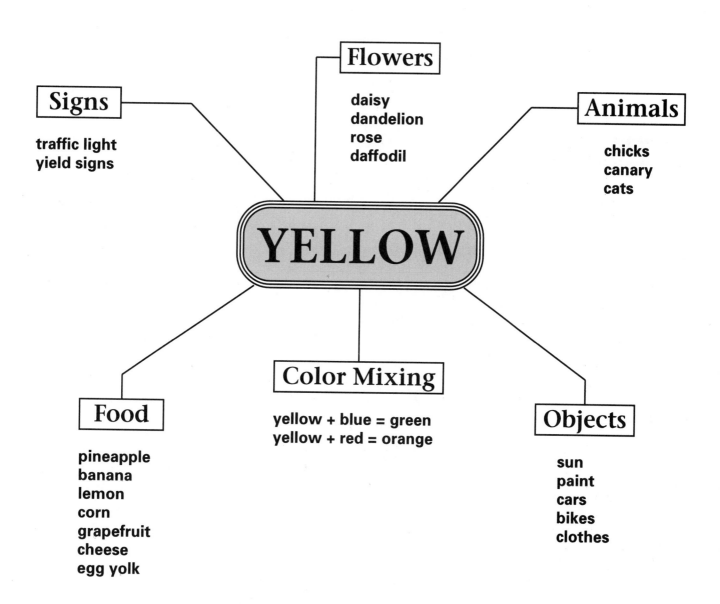

Signs

traffic light
yield signs

Flowers

daisy
dandelion
rose
daffodil

Animals

chicks
canary
cats

YELLOW

Food

pineapple
banana
lemon
corn
grapefruit
cheese
egg yolk

Color Mixing

yellow + blue = green
yellow + red = orange

Objects

sun
paint
cars
bikes
clothes

Theme Goals:

Through participating in the experiences provided by this theme, the children may learn:

1. Yellow flowers.

2. Yellow traffic signs.

3. Yellow animals.

4. Yellow-colored foods.

5. Colors formed by adding yellow.

6. Yellow objects.

Concepts for the Children to Learn:

1. Yellow is a primary color.

2. Yellow mixed with blue makes green.

3. Yellow mixed with red makes orange.

4. The sun is a yellow color.

5. The middle color on a traffic light is yellow.

6. Daisies, dandelions, and daffodils are yellow flowers.

7. A canary is a yellow bird.

8. Pineapples, bananas, and corn are yellow foods.

9. Bikes, cars, and cats can be yellow.

Vocabulary:

1. **yellow**—a primary color.

2. **primary colors**—red, blue, and yellow.

Bulletin Board

The purpose of this bulletin board is to have the children match the shapes, providing practice in visual discrimination. To prepare the bulletin board, collect yellow tagboard, a black felt-tip marker, scissors, yellow string, and push pins. Using yellow tagboard, draw sets of different-shaped balloons as illustrated. Outline with a black felt-tip marker and cut out. Take one from each set and attach to the top of the bulletin board. Staple a yellow string to hang from each balloon. Next, attach the remaining balloons on the bottom of the bulletin board. A push pin can be fastened next to each balloon, and the children can match the balloons by shape.

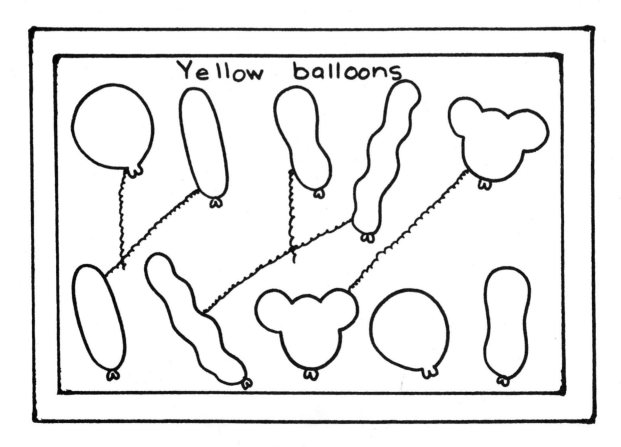

Parent Letter

Dear Parents,

Colors are such a big part of our world. Consequently, our new theme will focus on the color yellow. Throughout this week, the children will become aware of the color in their environment. It should be a bright time discovering the color yellow!

At School

Some learning experiences planned for the unit include:

- making scrambled eggs.
- visiting a paint store.
- learning the fingerplay, "Six Yellow Chickadees."
- making yellow soap crayons.
- playing with corn kernels in the sensory table.

At Home

At school we will be making yellow playdough. The children enjoy helping prepare the playdough and, of course, playing with it! It would be great fun for them to make it at home and they will be exposed to the mathematical concepts of amounts, fractions, and measurements. Here is the recipe:

2 cups flour
1 cup of salt
1 cup of water
2 tablespoons cooking oil
food coloring

Let your child assist in gathering and measuring the ingredients. Then mix all the ingredients together. To encourage play, provide some tools for your child to use: rolling pins, cookie cutters, spatulas, or potato mashers. Have fun!

Enjoy your child!

The yolk of an egg is yellow in color.

Fingerplays:

SIX YELLOW CHICKADEES
(Suit the actions to the words.)

Six yellow chickadees sitting by a hive.
One flew away and then there were five.
Five yellow chickadees sitting by the door.
One flew away and then there were four.
Four yellow chickadees sitting in a tree.
One flew away and then there were three.
Three yellow chickadees sitting by my shoe.
One flew away and then there were two.
Two yellow chickadees sitting by my thumb.
One flew away and then there was one.
One yellow chickadee flying around the sun.
He flew away and then there were none.

TEN FLUFFY CHICKENS

Five eggs and five eggs
   (hold up two hands)
That makes ten.

Sitting on top is the mother hen.
   (fold one hand over the other)
Crackle, crackle, crackle
   (clap hands three times)
What do I see?
Ten fluffy chickens
   (hold up ten fingers)
As yellow as can be!

Science:

1. **Paper Towel Dip**

   Fold a paper towel in half several times. Dip the towel into red water and then into yellow water. Open the towel carefully and allow it to dry. Orange designs will appear on the paper towel.

2. **Carnation Coloring**

   Put a carnation into a glass of water that has been dyed yellow with food coloring. Soon the carnation will show yellow streaks. During the summer other white garden flowers can be substituted.

3. **Yellow Soap Crayons**

   Measure one cup of mild powdered laundry soap. Add one tablespoon of food coloring. Add water by the teaspoonful until the soap is in liquid form. Stir well. Pour the soap into ice cube trays. Set in a sunny, dry place until hard. Soap crayons are great for writing in the sink, tub, or sensory table.

Dramatic Play:

Paint Store

Set up a paint store by including paint caps, paintbrushes, pans, rollers, drop cloths, paint clothes, a cash register, and play money.

Arts and Crafts:

1. **Yellow Paint**

   Provide yellow fingerpaint and yellow tempera paint in the art area.

2. **Corncob Painting**

   Cover the bottom of a shallow pan with thick yellow tempera paint. Using a corncob as an applicator, apply paint to paper.

3. **Popsicle Stick Prints**

   Cover the bottom of a shallow pan with thick yellow tempera paint. Apply the paint to paper using a popsicle stick as an applicator.

4. **Yellow Playdough**

   Combine two parts flour, one part salt, one part water, and two tablespoons cooking oil. Add yellow food coloring. Mix well. If prepared dough becomes sticky, add more flour.

5. **Baker's Clay**

   Combine 4 cups flour, 1 cup salt, and $1\frac{1}{2}$ cups water. Mix the ingredients. The children can shape forms. Place the forms on a cookie sheet and bake at 350 degrees for about 1 hour. The next day the children can paint the objects yellow.

6. **Yarn and Glue Designs**

   Provide yellow yarn, glue, and paper for the children to make their own designs.

7. **Record Player Designs**

   Punch a hole in the middle of a paper plate and place on the turntable of a record player. Turn the record player on. As the turntable spins around, the children can apply color by holding a yellow felt-tip marker on the paper plate. Interesting designs can be made.

Sensory:

1. **Shaving Cream Fun**

   Spray the contents of one can of shaving cream in the sensory table. Color the shaving cream by adding yellow food coloring.

2. **Corn Kernels**

   Place corn kernels in the sensory table.

3. **Yellow Goop**

   In the sensory table, mix one cup cornstarch, one cup water, and yellow food coloring. Mix together well.

4. **Water Toys**

   Add yellow food coloring to three inches of water in the sensory table. Provide water toys as accessories to encourage play during self-selected play activites.

Field Trips:

1. **Paint Store**

   Visit a paint store and observe the different shades of yellow. Collect samples of paint for use in the art area. If possible, also observe the manager mix yellow paint.

2. **Yellow in Our World**

   Take a walk and look for yellow objects. When you return to the classroom, prepare a language experience chart.

3. **Greenhouse**

   Visit a greenhouse and observe the different kinds of yellow flowers.

Math:

Sorting Shapes

   Cut circles, triangles, and rectangles out of yellow tagboard. Place on the math table. The children can sort the yellow shapes into groups. For younger children, the objects can be cut from different colors. Then the objects can be sorted by color.

Social Studies:

Tasting Party

   Cut a banana, a pineapple, a lemon, and a piece of yellow cheese into small pieces. Let the children sample each during snack time. The concept of color, texture, and taste can all be discussed.

Group Time (games, language):

Guessing Game: What's Missing?

Use any yellow familiar objects or toys that can be easily handled. The number will depend upon developmental appropriateness. For two-year-olds choose only two objects. On the other hand several objects can be used for five-year-olds. Spread them out on the floor and ask children to name each item. Then ask the group to close their eyes. Remove one item. When the group opens their eyes, ask them to tell you which item is missing.

Cooking:

1. **Banana Bobs**

   Cut bananas into chunks and dip into honey. Next roll in wheat germ and use large tooth-picks for serving.

2. **Carribean Banana Salad**

   3 green (unripe) bananas, peeled
   2 cups water
   1 teaspoon salt
   2 medium carrots, shredded
   1 small cucumber, sliced
   1 medium tomato, chopped
   1 avocado, cubed
   1 stalk celery, sliced
   vinaigrette dressing

   Heat bananas, water, and salt to boiling; reduce heat. Cover and simmer until bananas are tender, about 5 minutes. Drain and cool. Cut bananas crosswise into 1/2-inch slices. Toss bananas and remaining ingredients with vinaigrette dressing.

   Source: *Betty Crocker's International Cookbook.* (1980). New York: Random House.

3. **Corn Bread**

   1 cup flour
   1 cup cornmeal
   2 tablespoons sugar
   4 teaspoons baking powder
   1 teaspoon salt
   1 cup milk
   1/4 cup cooking oil or melted shortening
   1 egg, slightly beaten

   Preheat oven to 425 degrees. Grease (not oil) an 8- or 9-inch square pan. In medium mixing bowl, combine the dry ingredients. Stir in the remaining ingredients, beating by hand until just smooth. Pour batter into prepared pan. Bake for 20 to 25 minutes or until toothpick inserted in center comes out clean.

Multimedia:

The following resources can be found in educational catalogs:

1. Palmer, Hap. "Colors," *Learning Basic Skills through Music—Volume 1* [record].

2. Caspell, Jerry. *Color Me a Rainbow* [record].

3. *There's Music in the Colors* [record]. Kimbo Records.

Books:

The following books can be used to complement the theme:

1. Felix, Monique. (1991). *Colors*. New York: Stewart, Tabori, and Chang.

2. Lundell, Margaretta. (1989). *The Land of Colors*. New York: Putnam.

3. Morrison, Blake. (1987). *The Yellow House*. San Diego: Harcourt, Brace, Jovanovich.

4. Cox, Molly. (1988). *Louella & the Yellow Balloon*. New York: Harper Collins.

5. Van Fleet, Matthew. (1992). *One Yellow Lion: Fold-out Fun with Numbers, Colors, Animals*. New York: Dial Books for Young Readers.

6. Rogers, Alan. (1990). *Yellow Hippo*. Milwaukee, WI: Gareth Stevens, Inc.

7. Imershein, Betsy. (1989). *Finding Red Finding Yellow*. San Diego: Harcourt Brace Jovanovich.

8. Woolfitt, Gabrielle. (1992). *Yellow*. Minneapolis: Carolrhoda Books.

9. Bang, Molly. (1991). *Yellow Ball*. New York: Morrow Junior Books.

10. Mazer, Anne. (1990). *Yellow Button*. New York: Alfred A. Knopf Books for Young Readers.

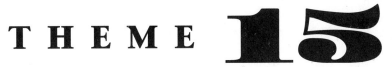

Other

homemaker
unemployed
seasonal
part-time
self-employed
shift
cottage
migrant

Construction

carpenter
plumber
cabinetmaker
architect

Transportation

taxi driver
bus driver
car salesperson
pilot
ambulance driver
truck driver
gas station attendant
astronaut

Service Workers

teacher
librarian
waitress/waiter
banker
cashier
custodian
secretary
auto mechanic
butcher
clerk
sanitation engineer

OCCUPATIONS

Production

farmer
factory worker
cook/chef
baker
miner

Health

doctor
nurse
dentist
hygienist
paramedic
child care

Communications

computer operator
television reporter
telephone operator
newspaper reporter
actor

Community Helpers

police officer
fire fighter
mail carrier
judge

Sports

announcer
umpire
coach
athlete

Theme Goals:

Through participating in the experiences provided by this theme, the children may learn:

1. Occupations of community helpers.

2. Sports figure occupations.

3. Health occupations.

4. Transportation occupations.

5. Communications occupations.

6. Construction occupations.

7. Production occupations.

8. Service occupations.

Concepts for the Children to Learn:

1. An occupation is a job a person performs.

2. There are many different kinds of occupations.

3. Taxi drivers, pilots, and ambulance drivers are transportation occupations.

4. Doctors, nurses, and dentists are health occupations.

5. A community helper is someone who helps us.

6. Teachers, librarians, and custodians are service occupations.

7. Cooks, factory workers, and farmers are production occupations.

8. Football and baseball players are sports occupations.

9. Television and newspaper reporters are in communications occupations.

10. Builders and architects are in construction occupations.

Vocabulary:

1. **occupation**—the job a person performs to earn money.

2. **job**—type of work.

3. **service**—helping people.

Bulletin Board

The purpose of this bulletin board is to stress that men and women can be doctors, farmers, construction workers, teachers, judges, etc. To prepare the bulletin board, construct a boy and girl out of tagboard. Design several occupational outfits that may be worn by either sex. Color and laminate the pieces. Magnet pieces or push pins and holes could be used to affix clothing on children.

Dress us for work.

Parent Letter

Dear Parents,

Hello! We will be exploring a new unit on occupations. Through experiences provided by this theme, the children will become aware of a great number of occupations and the way these workers help us today.

At School

Some learning experiences include:

- listening to books and records about people in our neighborhoods.
- making occupation hats.
- visiting a police station on Wednesday at 2:00 p.m. Join us if you can!
- observing an ambulance and talking with a paramedic.
- designing a job chart for our classroom.

At Home

Page through magazines with your child. Discuss equipment and materials that are used in various occupations. Questions such as the following can be asked to stimulate thinking skills: Who might use a typewriter to perform a job? What occupations involve the use of a cash register? Your child might be interested in visiting your place of employment!

Enjoy your child!

Abduraham likes cookies; someday he wants to be a bakery chef.

Fingerplays:

FARM CHORES

Five little farmers woke up with the sun.
  (hold up hand, palm forward)
It was early morning and the chores must be done.
The first little farmer went out to milk the cow.
  (hold up hand, point to thumb)
The second little farmer thought he'd better plow.
  (hold up hand, point to index finger)
The third little farmer cultivated weeds.
  (point to middle finger)
The fourth little farmer planted more seeds.
  (point to fourth finger)
The fifth little farmer drove his tractor round.
  (point to last finger)
Five little farmers, the best that can be found.
  (hold up hand)

TRAFFIC POLICEMAN

The traffic policeman holds up his hand.
  (hold up hand, palm forward)
He blows the whistle,
  (pretend to blow whistle)
He gives the command.
  (hold up hand again)
When the cars are stopped
  (hold up hand again)
He waves at me.
Then I may cross the street, you see.
  (wave hand as if indicating for someone to go)

THE CARPENTER

This is the way he saws the wood
  (right hand saws left palm)
Sawing, sawing, sawing.
This is the way he nails a nail
  (pound right fist on left palm)
Nailing, nailing, nailing.
This is the way he paints the house
  (right hand paints left palm)
Painting, painting, painting.

Dramatic Play:

1. **Hat Shop**

Police officer hats, fire fighter hats, construction worker hats, business person hats, and other occupation-related hats should be placed in the dramatic play area.

2. Classroom Cafe

Cover the table in the dramatic play area with a tablecloth, provide menus, a tablet for the waitress to write on, a space for a cook, etc. A cash register and play money may also be added to encourage play.

3. Hairstylist

Collect empty shampoo bottles, combs, barrettes, ribbons, hair spray containers, and magazines. Cut the cord off a discarded hair dryer and curling iron and place in the dramatic play area.

4. Our Library

Books on a shelf, a desk for the librarian, stamper and ink pad to check out books should be placed in the dramatic play area. A small table for children to sit and read their books would also add interest.

5. Workbench

A hammer, nails, saws, vises, a carpenter's apron, etc., should be added to the workbench. Eye goggles for the children's safety should also be included. Constant supervision is needed for this activity.

6. An Airplane

Create an airplane out of a large cardboard refrigerator box. If desired, the children can paint the airplane.

7. Post Office

A mailbox, letters, envelopes, stamps, and mail carrier bags can be set up in the dramatic play or art area.

8. Fast-Food Restaurant

Collect bags, containers, and hats to set up a fast-food restaurant.

9. A Construction Site

Hard hats, nails, a hammer, large blocks, and scrap wood can be provided for outdoor play. Cardboard boxes and masking tape should also be available.

10. Prop Boxes

The following prop boxes can be made by collecting the materials listed.

Police Officer

- badge
- hat
- uniform
- whistle
- walkie-talkie

Mail Carrier

- letter bag
- letter/stamps
- uniform
- mailbox
- envelopes
- paper
- pencil
- rubber stamp
- ink pad
- wrapped cardboard boxes

Fire Fighter

- boots
- helmet
- hose
- uniform
- gloves
- raincoat
- suspenders
- goggles

Doctor

- stethoscope
- medicine bottles
- adhesive tape
- cotton balls
- Red Cross armband
- chart holder

Arts and Crafts:

1. Mail Truck

Pre-cut mail truck parts including: 1 rectangle, 1 square, and 2 circles. The children can paste the pieces together and decorate. This activity is most appropriate for older children.

2. Occupation Vests

Cut a circle out of the bottom of a large paper grocery bag. Then from the circle cut a slit down the center of the bag. Cut out arm holes. Provide felt-tip colored markers for the children to decorate the vests. They may elect to be a pilot, police officer, mail carrier, baker, flight attendant, doctor, fire fighter, etc.

3. Mail Pouch

Cut the top half off a large grocery bag. Use the cutaway piece to make a shoulder strap. Staple it to the bag. The children can decorate the bag with crayons or markers.

Sensory:

The following materials can be added to the sensory table:

- sponge hair rollers with water
- wood shavings with scoops and scales
- sand with toy cars, trucks, airplanes
- pipes with water

Large Muscle:

Cut large cardboard boxes to make squad cars. Take the boxes and spray paint them either blue or white. Emblems can be constructed for the sides.

Field Trips/Resource People:

1. Take field trips to the following:

- bank
- library
- grocery store
- police station
- doctor/dentist office
- beauty salon/barber

- courthouse
- television/radio station
- airport
- farm
- restaurant

2. Invite the following resource people to school:

- police officer with squad car
- fire fighter with truck
- ambulance driver with ambulance
- truck driver with truck
- taxi driver with cab
- librarian with books

Social Studies:

1. Occupation Pictures

Pin occupation pictures on classroom bulletin boards and walls.

2. A Job Chart

Make a chart containing classroom jobs. Include tasks such as feeding the class pet, watering plants, sweeping the floor, wiping tables, etc.

Group Time (games, language):

1. Brushes as Tools

Collect all types of brushes and place in a bag. The children can reach into the bag and feel one. Before removing it, the child describes the kind of brush. When using with younger children, limit the number of brushes. Also, before placing the brushes in the bag, show the children each brush and discuss its use.

2. Machines as Helpers Chart

Machines and tools help people work and play. Ask the children to think of all of the machines they or their parents use around the house. As they name a machine, list it on a chart and discuss how it is used.

3. Mail It

Play a variation of "Duck, Duck, Goose." The children can sit in a circle. One child holds an envelope and walks around the circle saying, "letter," and taps each child on the head. When he gets to the one he wants to chase him, have the child drop the letter and say, "Mail it!" Then both children run around the circle until they return to the letter. The chaser gets to "mail" the letter by walking around and repeating the game.

Cooking:

Cheese Treats

cheese chunks
pretzel sticks

Cut cheese into small squares. Poke a pretzel into each cheese chunk.

Source: Wilmes, Liz & Dick. *Everyday Circle Times*. Illinois: Building Block Publications.

EXCURSIONS

Special excursions and events in an early childhood program give opportunities for widening the young child's horizons by providing children exciting direct experiences. The following places or people are some suggestions:

train station	tree farm	airport
dentist office	car wash	riding stable
post office	children's houses	barber shop
grocery store	garage mechanic	college dormitory
zoo	television studio	shoe repair shop
dairy	drugstore	print shop
family garden	bakery	artist's studio
poultry house	hospital	bowling alley
construction site	meat market	department store windows
beauty shop	library	potter's studio
offices	apple orchard	teacher's house
animal hospital	farm	street repair site
fire station		

Multimedia:

The following resources can be found in educational catalogs:

1. Rogers, Fred. *These are the People in My Neighborhood* [record].

2. *We All Live Together*. [record] Youngheart Records.

3. Jenkins, Ella. *My Street Begins at My House* [record].

4. Palmer, Hap. *Pretend* [record].

Books:

The following books can be used to complement the theme:

1. Lillegard, Dee. (1987). *I Can Be a Secretary*. Chicago: Children's Press.

2. Durham, Robert. (1987). *World At Work*. Chicago: Children's Press.

3. Merriam, Eve. (1991). *Daddies at Work*. New York: Simon and Schuster Trade.

4. Merriam, Eve. (1991). *Mommies at Work*. New York: Simon and Schuster Trade.

5. Civardi, Anne. (1986). *Things People Do*. Tulsa, OK: EDC Publishing.

6. Imershein, Betsy. (1990). *The Work People Do* (3 books). New York: Simon and Schuster Trade.

7. Moncure, Jane B. (1987). *What Can We Play Today?* Mankato, MN: Child's World, Inc.

8. Butterworth, Nick. (1992). *Busy People*. Cambridge, MA: Candlewick Press.

9. Grossman, Patricia. (1991). *The Night Ones*. San Diego: Harcourt Brace Jovanovich.

10. Hazen, Barbara Shook. (1992). *Mommie's Office*. New York: Macmillan.

11. Pringle, Laurence. (1989). *Jesse Builds a Road*. New York: Macmillan.

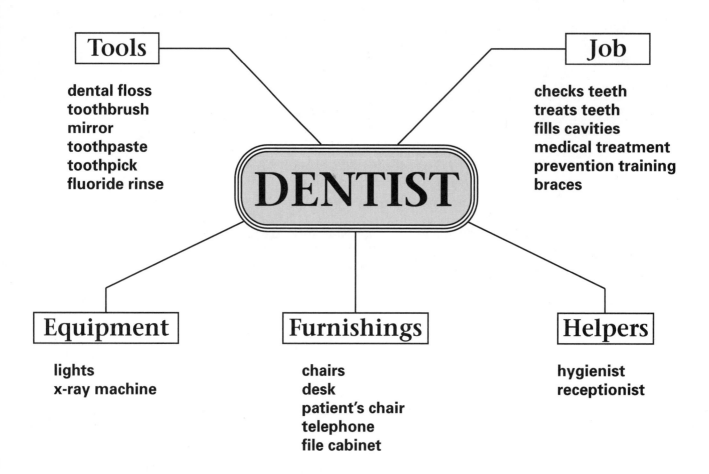

Tools

dental floss
toothbrush
mirror
toothpaste
toothpick
fluoride rinse

Job

checks teeth
treats teeth
fills cavities
medical treatment
prevention training
braces

DENTIST

Equipment

lights
x-ray machine

Furnishings

chairs
desk
patient's chair
telephone
file cabinet

Helpers

hygienist
receptionist

Theme Goals:

Through participating in the experiences provided by this theme, the children may learn:

1. How the dentist helps us.

2. Dentist's tools.

3. The name of a dental assistant.

4. Proper tooth care.

5. Dental equipment.

6. Dental office furnishings.

Concepts for the Children to Learn:

1. The dentist helps keep our teeth healthy.

2. Teeth are used to chew food.

3. Teeth should be brushed after each meal.

4. A hygienist helps the dentist.

5. A dentist removes decay from our teeth.

6. Pictures of our teeth are called x-rays.

7. A toothbrush and paste are used to clean teeth.

8. Dental floss helps clean between teeth.

9. The dentist's office has special machines.

Vocabulary:

1. **toothbrush**—a brush to clean teeth.

2. **toothpaste**—a paste to clean our teeth.

3. **dentist**—a person who helps keep our teeth healthy.

4. **teeth**—used to chew food.

5. **hygienist**—the dentist's assistant.

6. **cavity**—tooth decay.

7. **toothpick**—a stick-like tool used for removing food parts between our teeth.

8. **dental floss**—a string used to clean between the teeth.

Bulletin Board

The purpose of this bulletin board is to develop a positive self-concept and assist in name recognition. Prepare an attendance bulletin board by constructing a toothbrush out of tagboard for each student and teacher. See the illustration. Color the toothbrushes and print the children's names on them! Laminate. Punch holes in each toothbrush. Observe who brushed by observing who hung their toothbrush on a push pin on the bulletin board.

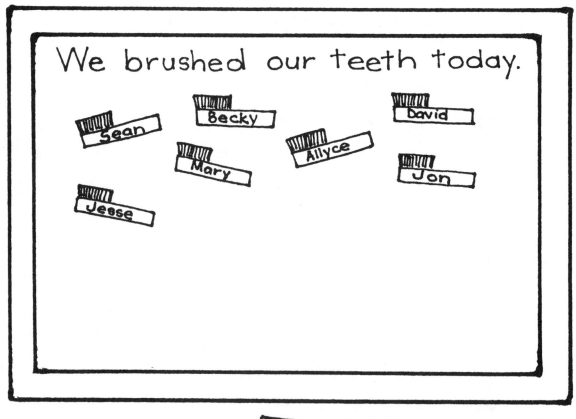

Parent Letter

Dear Parents,

We are continuing our study of community helpers with a unit on the dentist. The dentist is an important helper for us because our teeth are very important. Children are very aware of their teeth at this age. Many of the older five-year-olds will soon begin losing their baby teeth. Through the experiences provided in this unit, the children may learn that the dentist is a person who helps us to keep our teeth healthy. They will also spend some time learning about the importance of tooth care.

At School

Some of the experiences planned for the unit include:

* making toothpaste.
* string painting with dental floss at the art table.
* painting with discarded toothbrushes at the easel.
* exploring tools that a dentist uses.

Special Visitor

On Tuesday, January 13, we will meet Mrs. Jones, the dental hygienist at Dr. Milivitz's dental clinic. Mrs. Jones will discuss proper toothbrushing and will pass out toothbrush kits. You are invited to join our class at 10:00 a.m. for her visit.

At Home

Good habits start young! Dental cavities are one of the most prevalent diseases among children. It has been estimated that 98 percent of school-aged children have at least one cavity. You and your child can spend some time each day brushing your teeth together. Sometimes a child will more effectively brush if someone else is with him. It is important for children to realize that they are the primary caretakers of their teeth!

Have fun with your child!

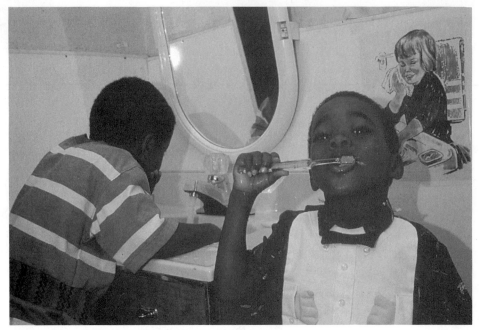

Children usually enjoy brushing their teeth.

Music:

1. **"Brushing Teeth"**
    (Sing to the tune of "Mulberry Bush")

    This is the way we brush our teeth,
    brush our teeth, brush our teeth.
    This is the way we brush our teeth,
    so early in the morning.

2. **"Clean Teeth"**
    (Sing to the tune of "Row, Row, Row Your Boat")

    Brush, brush, brush your teeth
    Brush them everyday.
    We put some toothpaste on our brush
    To help stop tooth decay.

Fingerplays:

MY TOOTHBRUSH

I have a little toothbrush.
    (use pointer finger)

I hold it very tight.
    (make hand into fist)
I brush my teeth each morning,
and then again at night.
    (use pointer finger and pretend to brush)

MY FRIEND THE TOOTHBRUSH

My toothbrush is a tool.
I use it every day.
I brush and brush and brush and brush
to keep the cavities away.
    (pretend to brush teeth)

Science:

1. **Tools**

    Place some safe dental products on the sensory table. Include a mirror, dental floss, toothbrush, toothpaste, etc. A dentist may even lend you a model of a set of teeth.

2. **Acid on Our Teeth**

    Show the children how acid weakens the enamel of your teeth. Place a hard-boiled egg

144

into a bowl of vinegar for 24 hours. Observe how the egg shell becomes soft as it decalcifies. The same principle applies to our teeth if the acid is not removed by brushing. (This activity is only appropriate with older children.)

3. **Making Toothpaste**

In individual plastic bags, place 4 teaspoons of baking soda, 1 teaspoon salt, and 1 teaspoon water. Add a drop of food flavoring extract such as peppermint, mint, or orange. The children can mix their own toothpaste.

4. **Sugar on Our Teeth**

Sugar found in sweet food can cause cavities on tooth enamel if it is not removed by rinsing or brushing. To demonstrate the effect of brushing, submerge white eggshells, which are made of enamel, into a clear glass of cola for 24 hours. Observe the discoloration of the eggshell. Apply toothpaste to toothbrush. Brush the eggshell removing the stain. Ask the children, "What caused the stain?"

Arts and Crafts:

1. **Easel Ideas**

   • paint with discarded toothbrushes
   • paint on tooth-shaped easel paper

2. **Toothbrushes and Splatter Screen**

Provide construction paper, splatter screens, and discarded toothbrushes. The children can splatter paint onto the paper using the toothbrush as a painting tool.

3. **Dental Floss Painting**

Provide thin tempera paint, paper, and dental floss. The child can spoon a small amount of paint onto their paper and can hold on to one end of the dental floss while moving the free end through the paint to make a design.

Sensory:

Additions to the Sensory Table

• toothbrushes and water
• peppermint extract added to water

Large Muscle:

1. **Drop the Toothbrush**

Set a large plastic open-mouth bottle on the floor. Encourage the children to try to drop the toothbrushes into the mouth of the bottle.

2. **Sugar, Sugar, Toothbrush**

Play like "Duck, Duck, Goose." The toothbrush tries to catch the "sugar" before it gets around the circle to where the "toothbrush" was sitting. Game can continue until interest diminishes.

Field Trips/Resource People:

1. **The Dentist**

Visit the dentist's office. Observe the furnishings and equipment.

2. **The Hygienist**

Invite a dental hygienist to visit the classroom. Ask the hygienist to discuss tooth care and demonstrate proper brushing techniques. After the discussion, provide each child with a disclosing tablet to check their brushing habits.

Group Time (games, language):

Pass the Toothpaste

Play music and pass a tube of toothpaste around the circle. When the music stops, the person who is holding the toothpaste stands up and claps his hands three times (or some similar action). Repeat the game.

Cooking:

1. Happy Teeth Snacks

- apple wedges
- orange slices
- asparagus
- cheese chunks
- milk
- cucumber slices
- cauliflower pieces

2. Smiling Apples

apples, cored and sliced
peanut butter
mini-marshmallows, raisins, or peanuts

Spread peanut butter on one side of each apple slice. Place 3 to 4 mini-marshmallows, raisins, or peanuts on the peanut butter of one apple slice. Top with another apple slice, peanut butter side down.

Multimedia:

The following resources can be found in educational catalogs:

1. Kangaroo, Captain. *Let's Go to the Dentist* [record]. Columbia.

2. Palmer, Hap. "Brush Away" on *Health and Safety* [record].

3. Raffi. "Brush Your Teeth" on *Singable Songs for the Very Young* [record]. Kimbo.

Books:

The following books can be used to complement the theme:

1. Quinlan, Patricia. (1992). *Brush Them Bright*. New York: Walt Disney Books Publishing Group.

2. Borgardt, Marianne. (1991). *Going to the Dentist*. New York: Simon and Schuster Trade.

3. Rogers, Fred. (1989). *Going to the Dentist*. New York: Putnam Publishing Group.

4. Mitra, Annie. (1990). *Tusk! Tusk!* New York: Holiday House Inc.

5. Luttrell, Ida. (1992). *Milo's Toothache*. New York: Dial Books for Young Readers.

6. McPhail, David. (1986). *The Bear's Toothache*. New York: Live Oak Media.

7. Kroll, Steven. (1992). *Loose Tooth*. New York: Scholastic Inc.

8. Linn, Margot. (1988). *A Trip to the Dentist*. New York: Harper Collins.

9. Pohl, Linda. (1991). *The Wiggly Tooth Book*. L. P. Pohl.

10. West, Colin. (1988). *The King's Toothache*. New York: Harper Collins.

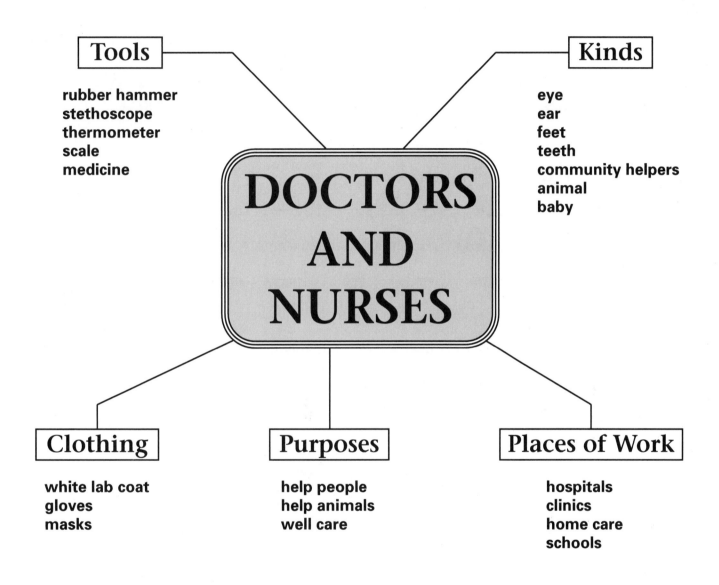

Tools

rubber hammer
stethoscope
thermometer
scale
medicine

Kinds

eye
ear
feet
teeth
community helpers
animal
baby

DOCTORS AND NURSES

Clothing

white lab coat
gloves
masks

Purposes

help people
help animals
well care

Places of Work

hospitals
clinics
home care
schools

Theme Goals:

Through participating in the experiences provided by this theme, the children may learn:

1. Kinds of doctors and nurses.

2. Places doctors and nurses work.

3. Tools used by doctors and nurses.

4. Clothing worn by doctors and nurses.

5. How doctors and nurses help people and animals.

Concepts for the Children to Learn:

1. A man or woman can be a doctor or nurse.

2. Doctors and nurses are community helpers.

3. Doctors and nurses help to keep people and animals healthy.

4. Doctors and nurses work in hospitals and clinics.

5. Lab coats, gloves, and masks are clothing doctors and nurses may wear.

6. Special doctors and nurses care for our eyes, ears, feet, and teeth.

7. A stethoscope is a tool used to check heartbeats and breathing.

8. Thermometers are used to check body temperature.

Vocabulary:

1. **doctor**—a man or woman who helps keep our bodies healthy.

2. **nurse**—a man or woman who usually assists the doctor.

3. **stethoscope**—a tool used for checking heartbeat and breathing.

4. **thermometer**—tool for checking body temperature.

5. **patient**—a person who goes to see a doctor.

6. **pediatrician**—a children's doctor.

7. **veterinarian**—an animal doctor.

8. **ophthalmologist**—an eye doctor.

Bulletin Board

The purpose of this bulletin board is to develop skills in identifying written numerals and matching sets to numerals. Construct bandages out of manilla tagboard as illustrated or use purchased adhesive bandages. Laminate. Collect small boxes and cover with white paper if necessary. The number will be dependent upon the developmental age of children. Plastic bandage boxes or 16-count crayon boxes may be used. On each box place a numeral. Affix the box to a bulletin board by stapling. The children can place the proper number of bandages in each box.

Parent Letter

Dear Parents,

I hope everyone in your family is happy and healthy! Speaking of healthy, we are starting a unit on doctors and nurses. The children will be learning about the different types of doctors and nurses and how they help people. They also will be introduced to some of the tools used by doctors and nurses.

At School

A few of the learning experiences planned include:
* listening to the story, *Tommy Goes to the Doctor*.
* taking our temperatures with forehead strips and recording them on a chart in the science area.
* dressing up as doctors and nurses in the dramatic play area.
* experimenting with syringes (no needles!) and water at the sensory table.

At Home

There are many ways to integrate this unit into your home. To begin, discuss the role of your family doctor. Talk about your child's visit to a physician. This will help to alleviate anxiety and fears your child may have about the procedures and setting.

Let your child help you prepare this nutritious snack at home. We will be making it for Wednesday's snack as well.

Peanut Butter Balls

1/2 cup peanut butter
1/2 cup honey
3/4 to 1 cup powdered milk

Combine all of the ingredients in a bowl. Shape the mixture into small balls and roll in chopped nuts, coconut, or graham cracker crumbs, if desired.

Model positive attitudes toward health for your child.

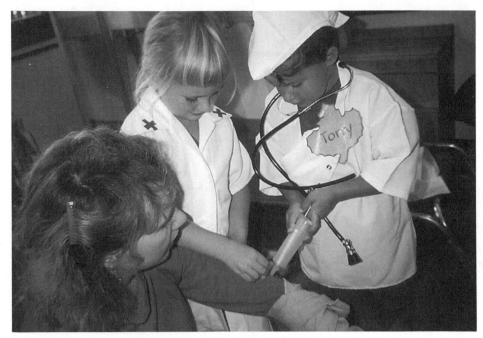

Girls and boys can be doctors or nurses.

Music:

1. **"The Doctor in the Clinic"**
   (Sing to the tune of "Farmer in the Dell")

   The doctor in the clinic.
   The doctor in the clinic.
   Hi-ho the derry-o,
   The doctor in the clinic.

   The doctor takes a nurse…
   The nurse takes a patient…
   The patient gets help…
   The patient gets better…

2. **"To the Hospital"**
   (Sing to the tune of "Frere Jacques")

   To the hospital, to the hospital,
   We will go, we will go.
   We will see the doctors,
   And we'll see the nurses,
   Dressed in white, dressed in white.

Fingerplays:

MISS POLLY'S DOLLY

Miss Polly had a dolly that was sick, sick, sick.
   (cradle arms and look sad)

She called for the doctor to come quick, quick, quick.
   (clap hands three times)
The doctor came with his coat and his hat.
   (point to your shirt and head)
And rapped on the door with a rap, rap, rap.
   (pretend to knock three times)
He looked at the dolly and he shook his head
   (shake head)
And he said, "Miss Polly, put her straight to bed."
   (shake finger)
Then he wrote on a paper for some pills, pills, pills.
   (hold left hand out flat, pretend to write with right hand)
I'll be back in the morning with my bill, bill, bill.
   (hold left hand out flat, wave it up and down as if waiting to be handed cash)

Note: The doctor may be male or female. Substitute pronouns.

DOCTOR DAY

My father said,
"It's doctor day,"
Then he and I
We're on our way
To see our friend

The doctor who
Would check me out
As doctors do.
She had more things
Than I can tell
To help her keep
The people well.
She checked me up
And all the while
She wore a big
And friendly smile.
So now I hope
That someday you
May go to see
The doctor too!

Source: Wilmes, Liz & Dick. (1983). *Everyday Circle Times*. Illinois: Building Blocks Publishing.

Science:

1. **Thermometer**

   Place a variety of unbreakable thermometers on the science table. Include a candy, meat, and an outdoor thermometer. Also include a strip thermometer that can be safely used on children's foreheads.

2. **Casts**

   Ask personnel at a local hospital to save clean, discarded casts. Place the casts on the science table, allowing the children to observe the materials, try them on for size, as well as feel their weight. The children may also enjoy decorating the casts.

3. **Stethoscope**

   Place a stethoscope on the science table for the children to experiment with. After each child uses it, wipe the ear plugs with alcohol to prevent the transmission of disease.

4. **Doctors' Tools**

   In a feely box place several tools that a doctor uses. Include a thermometer, gauze, stethoscope, rubber hammer, and a tongue depressor.

5. **Making Toothpaste**

   Mix four teaspoons baking soda, one teaspoon salt, and one teaspoon peppermint flavoring. Then add just enough water to form a thick paste.

Dramatic Play:

1. **Doctors and Nurses**

   Make a prop box for a doctor and nurse. Include a white coat, rubber gloves, a thermometer, gauze, tape, masks, eye droppers, tongue depressors, eye chart, cots, blankets, pencil and paper, empty and washed medicine bottles, a stethoscope, a scale, and syringes without needles. A first-aid kit including gauze and tape, bandages, butterflies, a sling, and ace bandages can be placed in this box. Place the prop boxes in the dramatic play area.

2. **Animal Clinic**

   Place stuffed animals with the doctor tools in the dramatic play area.

3. **Eye Doctor Clinic**

   Ask a local eye doctor for discontinued eye glass frames. Place the frames with a wall chart in the dramatic play area.

Arts and Crafts:

1. **Cotton Swab Painting**

   Place cotton swabs, cottonballs, and tempera paint on a table in the art area. The cotton swabs and balls can be used as painting tools.

2. **Body Tracing**

   Trace the children's bodies by having them lie down on a large piece of paper. The body shape can be decorated at school by the child with crayons and felt-tip markers. The shapes could also be taken home and decorated with parental assistance.

3. **Eye Dropper Painting**

Provide eye droppers, thin tempera paint, and absorbent paper. Designs can be made by using the eye dropper as a painting tool. Another method is to prepare water colored with food coloring in muffin tins. Using heavy paper towels with construction paper underneath for protection, the children will enjoy creating designs with the colored water.

Field Trips/Resource People:

1. **Doctor's Office**

Visit a doctor's office.

2. **Resource Person**

Invite a nurse or doctor to visit the classroom. Encourage them to talk briefly about their jobs. They can also share some of their tools with the children.

3. **The Hospital**

Visit a local hospital.

Math:

1. **Weight and Height Chart**

Prepare a height and weight chart out of tagboard. Record each child's height and weight on this chart. Repeat periodically throughout the year to note physical changes.

2. **Tongue Depressor Dominoes**

Make a set of dominoes by writing on tongue depressors. Divide each tongue depressor in half with a felt-tip marker. On each half place a different number of dots. Consider the children's developmental level in determining the number of dots to be included. Demonstrate to interested children how to play dominoes.

3. **Bandage Lotto**

Construct a bandage lotto game using various sizes and shapes of bandages. Place it on a table for use during self-selected activity time.

Social Studies:

Pictures

Display various health-related pictures in the room at the children's eye level, including doctors and nurses. Pictures should depict males and females in these health-related fields.

Group Time (games, language):

1. **Doctor, Doctor, Nurse**

Play "Duck, Duck, Goose" inserting the words, "Doctor, Doctor, Nurse."

2. **What's Missing?**

Place a variety of doctors' and nurses' tools on a large tray. Tell the children to close their eyes. Remove one item from the tray. Then have the children open their eyes and guess which item has been removed. Continue playing the game using all of the items as well as providing an opportunity for each child.

Cooking:

1. **Mighty Mixture**

Mix any of the following:
A variety of dried fruit (apples, apricots, pineapple, raisins)
A variety of seeds (pumpkin, sunflower)
A variety of nuts (almond, walnuts, pecans)

2. **Vegetable Juice**

Prepare individual servings of vegetable juice in a blender by adding 1/2 cup of cut-up vegetables and 1/4 cup water. Salt to taste. Vegetables that can be used include: celery, carrots, beets, tomatoes, cucumbers, and zucchini.

Books:

The following books can be used to complement the theme:

1. Reit, Seymour. (1984). *Jenny's in the Hospital*. Racine, WI: Western Publishing Company, Inc.

2. Rogers, Fred. (1986). *Going to the Doctor*. New York: G.P. Putnam's Sons.

3. Lumley, Kathryn Wentzel. (1985). *I Can Be an Animal Doctor*. Chicago: Children's Press.

4. Bauer, Judith. (1990). *What's It Like to Be a Doctor?* Mahwah, NJ: Troll Associates.

5. Fine, Anne. (1992). *Poor Monty*. Boston: Houghton Mifflin Co.

6. Bauer, Judith. (1990). *What's It Like to Be a Nurse?* Mahwah, NJ: Troll Associates.

7. Bauer, Judith. (1990). *Kevin and the School Nurse*. Mahwah, NJ: Troll Associates.

8. Davidson, Martine. (1992). *Maggie and the Emergency Room*. New York: Random House Books for Young Readers.

9. Davidson, Martine. (1992). *Rita Goes to the Hospital!* New York: Random House Books for Young Readers.

10. Bucknall, Caroline. (1991). *One Bear in the Hospital*. New York: Dial Books for Young Readers.

11. Rockwell, Anne. (1985). *The Emergency Room*. New York: Macmillan.

12. Kuklin, Susan. (1988). *Taking My Dog to the Vet*. New York: Macmillan.

13. Linn, Margot. (1988). *A Trip to the Doctor*. New York: Harper Collins.

Clothing

hats
coats
masks
boots
gloves
uniforms

Job

fight fires
inspect buildings
teach fire safety
provide medical treatment

Fire Station

garage
workroom
kitchen
bedroom
dalmatians

FIRE FIGHTERS

Safety

when to use
house
person
how to get them
false alarms
matches
cooking
smoking

Vehicles

fire trucks
water trucks
fire chief car
ambulance
police car

Equipment

fire hydrant
fire extinguisher
hose
nozzles
ax
ladders
telephone
communication radios
water

Theme Goals:

Through participating in the experiences provided by this theme, the children may learn:

1. The fire fighter's job.

2. Fire fighter's clothing.

3. Vehicles used by fire fighters.

4. Fire fighting equipment.

5. Areas inside of a fire station.

Concepts for the Children to Learn:

1. Men and women who fight fires are called fire fighters.

2. Fire fighters help keep our community safe.

3. Fire fighters wear special hats and clothing.

4. The fire station has a garage, kitchen, workroom, and sleeping rooms.

5. The fire station has a special telephone number.

6. Ladders and water hoses are needed to fight fires.

7. Fire and water trucks are driven to fires.

8. Fire fighters check buildings to make sure they are safe.

9. Fire fighters teach us fire safety.

10. Fire extinguishers can be used to put out small fires.

11. Fire drills teach us what to do in case of a fire.

Vocabulary:

1. **fire alarm**—a sound warning people about fire.

2. **fire drill**—practice for teaching people what to do in case of a fire.

3. **fire extinguisher**—equipment that puts out fires.

4. **hose**—a tube that water flows through.

5. **helmet**—a protective hat.

6. **fire engine**—trucks carrying tools and equipment needed to fight fires.

7. **fire station**—a building that provides housing for fire fighters and fire trucks.

156

Bulletin Board

The purpose of this bulletin board is to develop an awareness of clothing worn by fire fighters and to reinforce color matching skills. From tagboard construct five fire fighter hats. Color each hat a different color. Then construct five fire fighter boots from tagboard. Color coordinate boots to match the hats. Laminate all of the pieces. Staple hats in two rows across the top of the bulletin board as illustrated. Staple boots in a row across the bottom of the bulletin board. Affix matching yarn to each hat. Children can match each hat to its corresponding colored boot by winding the string around a push pin in the top of the boot.

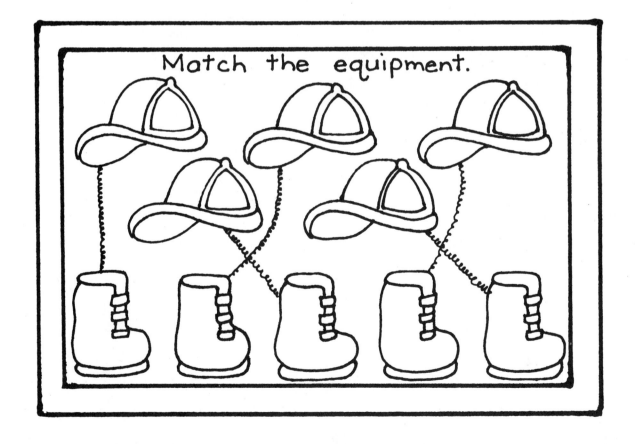

Parent Letter

Dear Parents,

Because next week is Fire Prevention Week, we have decided that it would be fun and educational to focus on some very important community helpers—fire fighters. The children will become more aware of the role of the fire fighter, clothing worn by fire fighters, and parts of the fire station. We will also be talking about how to use the telephone to call the emergency fire number.

At School

We have many activities planned for this unit! On Monday, we will paint a large box to create our own fire engine to use during the week in the dramatic play area. On Tuesday, a real fire engine will visit the parking lot, so the children can see how many tools fire fighters need to take along on the job. We'll also be making fire helmets, and practicing our fire drill procedures.

At Home

To ensure your family's safety, talk with your child about what would happen in the event of a fire at your house. You can do this calmly, without frightening your child. Practice taking a fire escape route from the child's bedroom, the playroom, kitchen, and other rooms of your house. Establish a meeting place so that family members can go to the same location in the event of a fire.

Enjoy your child as you share the importance of safety in the event of a fire.

A unit on fire fighters provides an opportunity to practice fire drills.

Music:

"Down By the Station"

Down by the station early in the morning
See the great big fire trucks all in a row.
Hear the jangly fire bell sound a loud alarm now—
Chug chug, clang clang, off we go!

Fingerplay:

TEN BRAVE FIRE FIGHTERS

Ten brave fire fighters sleeping in a row.
   (fingers curled to make sleeping men)
Ding, dong, goes the bell
   (pull down on the bell cord)
And down the pole they go.
   (with fists together make hands slide down
   the pole)
Off on the engine, oh, oh, oh!
   (pretend you are steering the fire engine
   very fast)
Using the big hose, so, so, so.
   (make a nozzle with fist to use hose)

When all the fire's out, home so slow.
Back to bed, all in a row.
   (curl all fingers again for sleeping fire
   fighters)

Source: Adapted from Cromwell, Liz, & Hibner, Dixie. (1976). *Finger Frolics*. Mt. Ranier, MD: Gryphon House.

Dramatic Play:

1. **Fire Fighters**

   Place fire fighting clothes such as hats, boots, and coats for children to wear. Sometimes fire station personnel will allow schools to borrow some of their clothing and equipment. Also, provide a bell to use as an alarm. A vacuum cleaner hose or a length of garden hose can be included to represent a water hose to extend play.

2. **Fire Truck**

   A fire truck can be cut from a cardboard refrigerator box. The children may want to paint the box yellow or red. A steering wheel and chairs may be added.

Arts and Crafts:

1. **Fire Fighters' Hats**

   Provide materials for the children to make fire hats. The hats can be decorated with foil, crayons, or paint. The emergency number 911 may be printed on the crown.

2. **Charcoal Drawings**

   Provide real charcoal at the easels to be used as an application tool.

3. **Crayon Melting**

   Place waxed crayons and paper on the art table for the children to create a design during self-initiated or self-directed play. Place a clean sheet of paper over the picture. Apply a warm iron. Show the children the effect of heat. This activity needs to be carefully supervised. The caption "crayon melting" may be printed on a bulletin board. On the board place the children's pictures, identifying each by name in the upper left-hand corner.

Sensory:

1. Fill the sensory table with water. Provide cups and rubber tubing to resemble hoses and funnels.

2. Place sand in the sensory table. Add fire engines, fire fighter dolls, popsicle sticks to make fences, and blocks to make buildings or houses.

Large Muscle:

1. **Fire Fighter's Workout**

   Lead children in a fire fighter's workout. Do exercises like jumping jacks, knee bends, leg lifts, and running in place. Ask children why they think fire fighters need to be in good physical condition for their jobs.

2. **Obstacle Course**

   Make an obstacle course. Let children follow a string or piece of tape under chairs or tables, over steps, and across ladders. This activity can be planned for indoors or outdoors.

Field Trips/Resource People:

1. **Fire Station**

   Take a trip to a fire station. Observe the clothing worn by fire fighters, the building, the vehicles, and the tools.

2. **Fire fighter**

   Invite a fire fighter to bring a fire truck to your school. Ask the fire fighter to point out the special features such as the hose, siren, ladders, light, and special clothing kept on the truck. If permissable and safe, let the children climb onto the truck.

Math:

1. **Sequencing**

   Cut a piece of rubber tubing into various lengths. The children can sequence the pieces from shortest to longest.

2. **Emergency Number**

   Contact your local telephone company for trainer telephones to use. If developmentally appropriate, teach the children how to dial a local emergency number.

Social Studies:

1. **Safety Rules**

   Discuss safety rules dealing with fire. Let children generate ideas about safety. Write their ideas on chart paper and display. Discuss why fire drills are a good idea.

2. **Fire Inspection Tour**

   Tour the classroom or building looking for fire extinguishers, emergency fire alarm boxes, and exits.

3. Fire Drill

Schedule a fire drill. Prior to the drill talk to the children about fire drill procedures.

Group Time (games, language):

Language Experience

Review safety rules. Write the rules on a large piece of paper. These rules can also be included in a parent letter as well as posted in the classroom.

Cooking:

Firehouse Baked Beans

Purchase canned baked beans. To the beans, add cut-up hot dogs and extra catsup. Heat and serve for snack.

Multimedia:

The following resources can be found in educational catalogs:

1. *Little Firemen* [record]. Young People's Records.

2. "Let's Be Firemen" on *Men Who Come to Our House* [record]. Young People's Records.

3. Poelker, Kathy Lecinski. "At the Firehouse" on *Look At My World* [record]. Look at Me Company.

Books:

The following books can be used to complement the theme:

1. Rey, Margaret, & Shalleck, Alan J. (1985). *Curious George at the Fire Station.* New York: Scholastic Inc.

2. Rius, Marie. (1985). *Fire.* Woodbury, NY: Barron's.

3. Maas, Robert. (1989). *Fire Fighters.* New York: Scholastic Inc.

4. Leonard, Marcia. (1990). *Jeffrey Lee, Future Fireman.* Morristown, NJ: Silver, Burdett and Ginn.

5. Marion, Kenneth P. (1990). *Volunteer Firefighter.* Kings Park, NY: JK Publishing.

6. Seymour, Peter. (1990). *Fire Fighters.* New York: Dutton Children's Books.

7. Barrett, Norman. (1991). *Picture World of Fire Engines.* New York: Watts, Franklin, Inc.

8. Pellowski, Michael. (1989). *Fire Fighter.* Tarrytown, NY: Troll Associates.

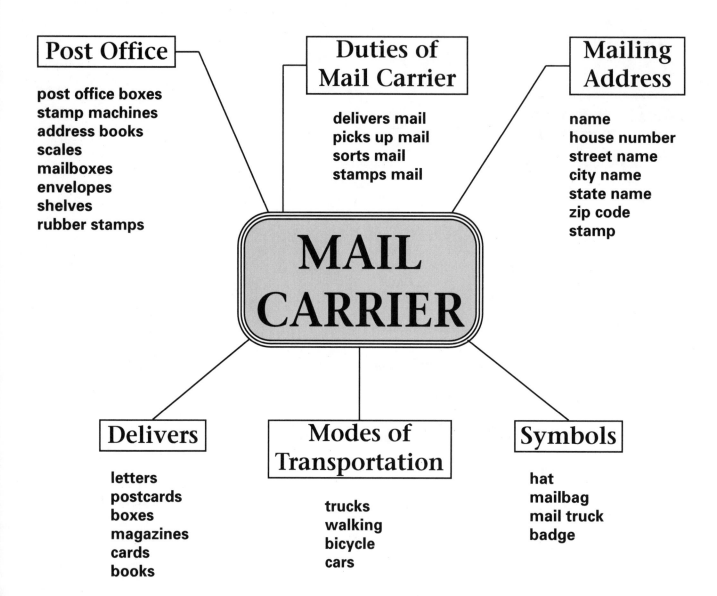

Post Office

post office boxes
stamp machines
address books
scales
mailboxes
envelopes
shelves
rubber stamps

**Duties of
Mail Carrier**

delivers mail
picks up mail
sorts mail
stamps mail

**Mailing
Address**

name
house number
street name
city name
state name
zip code
stamp

**MAIL
CARRIER**

Delivers

letters
postcards
boxes
magazines
cards
books

**Modes of
Transportation**

trucks
walking
bicycle
cars

Symbols

hat
mailbag
mail truck
badge

Theme Goals:

Through participating in the experiences provided by this theme, the children may learn:

1. Duties of a mail carrier.

2. Symbols identifying a mail carrier.

3. Objects found in a post office.

4. Parts of a mailing address.

5. Types of postal deliveries.

Concepts for the Children to Learn:

1. A man or woman who delivers mail is a mail carrier.

2. The mail carrier usually wears a badge and a hat.

3. A mail carrier sometimes drives a truck or jeep.

4. Mail carriers deliver cards, letters, postcards, boxes, books, and magazines.

5. Stamps are used for mailing.

6. Names, house numbers, street names, city names, state names, and zip codes are on mailing labels.

7. A post office has stamp machines, address books, mailboxes, and envelopes.

8. Scales are used to weigh mail.

Vocabulary:

1. **post office**—place where mail is sorted.

2. **letter**—a printed message.

3. **zip code**—the last numbers on a mailing address.

4. **address**—directions for the mail carrier.

5. **mail**—letters, cards, postcards, and packages.

6. **envelope**—a cover for a letter.

7. **stamp**—a sticker put on mail.

8. **mail carrier**—person who delivers mail.

9. **mailbag**—bag that holds letters and postcards.

Bulletin Board

The purpose of this bulletin board is to reinforce the mathematical skill of matching a set to its written numeral. Construct mailboxes out of tagboard. Each mailbox should include a flag, which is red-colored and contains a numeral. The number will depend upon the maturity of the children. A set of dots, corresponding to the numeral on the flag, should be placed on the mailbox. Hang the mailboxes on the bulletin board. Next, construct letters by using small cards with sets of dots on them. The children can match the dots on the cards with the dots and numerals on the mailboxes. If desired, magnet pieces can be attached to both the mailboxes and the cards.

Parent Letter

Dear Parents,

We have been busy discussing the roles of a variety of community helpers these past weeks. Next we will focus the curriculum on the role of the mail carrier. The children will be learning about letters, stamps, and addresses, and will be able to identify objects found in a post office. They will also become aware of how mail is delivered and what needs to be on a letter or package before it is delivered.

At School

Some of the many learning activities scheduled include:

- listening to the story, *Adventures of a Letter*, by Warren G. Schloat.
- playing in a post office set up in the classroom.
- making mailboxes and postcards.
- weighing letters and packages.
- delivering mail to our friends in our room.

At Home

Let your children help or watch you open the mail. Give your child the "junk mail" to play with. Show your child where your address is on your house and mailbox. You may also enjoy having your children dictate a letter to a grandparent, favorite aunt, or cousin. As you write the letter, show your child the printed alphabet letters to develop an awareness of alphabet letters. After you finish the letter, address an envelope. Let your child lick the stamp and show the proper placement. Then it's off to the post office!

Enjoy your child!

The mail used to be delivered by pony.

Music:

1. **"Mailing Letters"**
   (Sing to the tune of "The Mulberry Bush")

   This is the way we mail a letter,
   Mail a letter, mail a letter.
   This is the way we mail a letter,
   So early in the morning.

2. **"Let's Pretend"**
   (Sing to the tune of "Here We Are Together"
   and "Did You Ever See a Lassie")

   Let's pretend that we are mail carriers,
   Are mail carriers, are mail carriers.
   Let's pretend that we are mail carriers,
   We'll have so much fun.
   We'll carry the letters and put them in boxes.
   Let's pretend that we are mail carriers,
   We'll have so much fun.

Fingerplays:

LITTLE MAIL CARRIER

I am a little mail carrier
   (point to self)
Who can do nothing better.
I walk.
   (walk in place)
I run.
   (run in place)
I hop to your house.
   (hop in place)
To deliver your letter.

FIVE LITTLE LETTERS

Five little letters lying on a tray.
   (extend fingers of right hand)
Mommy came and took the first one away.
   (bend down thumb)
Daddy said, "This one's for me!"
I counted them twice, now there are three.
   (bend down pointer finger)
Brother Bill asked, "Did I get any mail?"
He found one and cried, "A letter from Gail."
   (bend down middle finger)
My sister Jane took the next to the last
And ran upstairs to open it fast.
   (bend down ring finger)
As I can't read, I am not able to see,
Whom the last one is for, but I hope it's for me!
   (wiggle last finger, clap hands)

THE MAIL CARRIER

I come from the post office
   (walk from post office)
My mail sack on my back.
   (pretend to carry sack on back)
I go to all the houses
   (pretend to go up to a house)
Leaving letters from my pack.
   (pretend to drop letters into mailbox)
One, two, three, four
   (hold up fingers as you count)
What are these letters for?
   (pretend to hold letters as you count)
One for John. One for Lou.
   (pretend to hand out letters)
One for Tom and one for you!
   (pretend to hand out letters to others)

166

LETTER TO GRANDMA

Lick them, stamp them
   (make licking and stamping motions)
Put them in a box.
   (extend arms outward)
Hope that Grandma
Loves them a lot!
   (hug self)

Dramatic Play:

1. **Post Office**

    Develop the dramatic play area into a post office. Provide a mailbox, mail carrier hats, mailbag, stamps, cash register, rubber date stamps, and a letter scale. The children may enjoy acting out the role of a mail carrier or a post office worker.

2. **Letters**

    Provide a variety of writing materials. Include different colors of paper, writing tools, and envelopes. The children can dictate a letter to a friend or a family member. After all interested children have completed dictation, apply stamps and walk to the nearest mailbox or post office. (Contact a local printer, office supply store, or card shop and ask for discontinued samples or misprinted envelopes.)

Science:

1. **Dress the Mail Carrier**

    Place flannel board pieces representing seasonal clothing for a mail carrier. Let the children select the appropriate clothing for the weather. This may be an interesting activity to introduce daily during group time.

2. **Weighing Mail**

    A variety of letters, boxes, stamps, and a scale can be placed in the science area. The children can weigh letters and packages. This activity can be extended by placing materials in the boxes and weighing them, noting the difference.

3. **How Does the Mail Feel?**

    Place different types of envelopes and stationery on the sensory table for the children to explore. Include airmail paper, onionskin, bond paper, typing paper, and different kinds of stationery. Also, provide a magnifying glass.

Field Trips/Resource People:

1. **Post Office**

    Plan a field trip to the local post office. Observe the mailboxes, stamp machines, address books, scales, and rubber stamps with the children. Mail a postcard back to the center. Count the number of days it takes to arrive.

2. **Mail Carrier**

    Invite the mail carrier who delivers mail or the local postmaster to your center or school to visit in the classroom. Ask the mail carrier to share his mailbag, hat, etc., with the children.

Social Studies:

Mailboxes

Plan a walk around the neighborhood. Observe the different types of mailboxes and addresses.

Math:

The number of items and numerals used in these activities needs to be adjusted to reflect the developmental appropriateness of the children.

1. **Dominoes**

    Create dominoes out of envelopes. Have the children match the numbers and dots.

2. **How Many Stamps?**

    Write an individual numeral on an envelope. Make or collect many stamps. The children can place the correct number of stamps in the envelope with the corresponding numeral. A variation of this activity is to make mailboxes from shoeboxes. Again, write a numeral on each box. Make or collect many different envelopes. The children can put the correct number of letters in the corresponding mailboxes.

3. **Package Seriation**

Prepare several packages and letters of different sizes. The children can place the letters and packages in order from largest to smallest or smallest to largest.

Arts and Crafts:

1. **Easel Ideas**

Cut easel paper in the shape of envelopes, letters, stamps, or mailbags.

2. **Postcards**

Have children make postcards at school to send to family and friends. Provide index cards. Let the children design the postcards.

3. **Mailboxes**

Make mailboxes out of old shoeboxes. Each child can decorate his own box. Names can be added by the child or teacher. Include a home address for older children.

4. **Mail Truck**

Construct a mail truck out of a large cardboard box. Provide paint for the children to decorate it. When dried, place chairs and, if available, a steering wheel inside for the children to drive.

5. **Stamps**

Collect assorted stamps or stickers. Cancelled stamps can be reglued. The children can make a stamp collage.

Group Time (games, language):

Thank You

Write a thank-you note to the postmaster or mail carrier after visiting.

Cooking:

Zip Code Special

1 1/2 cups nonfat dry milk
2 cups fresh or frozen berries
1 teaspoon vanilla
1 cup water
1 tray ice cubes

Blend all ingredients in a blender. Serve and enjoy.

Books:

The following books can be used to complement the theme:

1. Matthews, Morgan. (1990). *What's It Like to Be a Postal Worker?* Mahwah, NJ: Troll Associates.

2. Ziegler, Sandra. (1989). *A Visit to the Post Office.* Chicago: Children's Press.

3. Hedderwick, Mairi. (1988). *Kathie Morag Delivers the Mail.* New York: Little, Brown and Co.

4. Henri, Adrian. (1990). *The Postman's Palace.* New York: Macmillan Children's Book Group.

5. Skurzynski, Gloria. (1992). *Here Comes the Mail.* New York: Macmillan Children's Book Group.

6. Casely, Judith. (1991). *Dear Annie*. New York: Greenwillow Books.

7. Johnson, Jean. (1987). *Postal Workers: A to Z*. New York: Walker & Co.

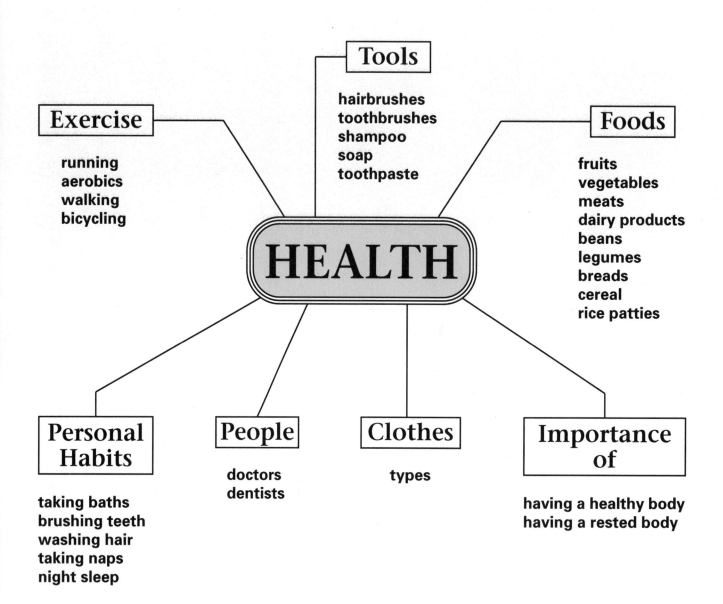

Tools

hairbrushes
toothbrushes
shampoo
soap
toothpaste

Exercise

running
aerobics
walking
bicycling

Foods

fruits
vegetables
meats
dairy products
beans
legumes
breads
cereal
rice patties

HEALTH

Personal Habits

taking baths
brushing teeth
washing hair
taking naps
night sleep

People

doctors
dentists

Clothes

types

Importance of

having a healthy body
having a rested body

Theme Goals:

Through participating in the experiences provided by this theme, the children may learn:

1. Importance of good health.

2. Health foods.

3. Exercise clothes.

4. Tools used for health needs.

5. Exercises for health.

6. Health habits.

7. Health occupations.

Concepts for the Children to Learn:

1. We need to take good care of our bodies.

2. Vitamins, shampoo, soap, and toothpaste are health aids.

3. Doctors and dentists provide health checkups.

4. Running, aerobics, and walking are all forms of exercise.

5. Fruits, vegetables, dairy products, beans, legumes, meat, breads, and cereals keep our bodies healthy.

6. Our bodies need rest.

7. Different types of clothing are worn during exercise.

8. Brushing teeth, washing hair, and bathing are ways to keep our bodies clean.

9. Hairbrushes and toothbrushes are health tools.

Vocabulary:

1. **exercise**—moving body parts.

2. **health**—feeling good.

3. **nutrition**—eating foods that are good for our body.

4. **cleanliness**—keeping our body parts free from dirt.

5. **diet**—the food we eat.

6. **checkup**—a visit to a doctor to make sure you are healthy.

Bulletin Board

The purpose of this bulletin board is to have the children match the health aids to their corresponding shadow. Construct health aids from white tagboard such as a toothbrush, toothpaste, comb, brush, and soap. Color the objects with colored felt-tip markers and laminate. Trace each of the health aids onto black construction paper to construct shadows as illustrated. Staple the shadow aids on the bulletin board either by affixing magnets or using push pins. Then punch a hole in the health aids for the children to hang them on the appropriate shadow.

Parent Letter

Dear Parents,

We will be starting a unit on health. This unit will include many aspects of health. We will be discussing foods that are good for us, important personal habits, and exercise. Through this unit the children will develop an awareness of how important it is to keep their bodies healthy.

At School

Some of the learning experiences planned for the week include:

- tracing our bodies at the art center.
- visiting Dr. Thomas, the dentist, at her office.
- having a visit by an aerobics instructor.
- creating healthy snacks.
- weighing and measuring ourselves.

Field Trip

Arrangements have been made to visit Dr. Thomas's office on Thursday of this week. Dr. Thomas will give us a tour of the dental clinic and show us various pieces of dental equipment. We will walk to her office, leaving school at 10:00 a.m., and return just in time for lunch. Please have your child at school by 10:00 a.m. if he wishes to participate. Parents, please feel free to join us.

Just a Reminder

If your child's toothbrush at school is missing, please send another one. We teach the importance of dental hygiene by brushing our teeth after all meals and snacks at school.

At Home

Cotton swabs may be used instead of brushes for painting. They may also be used to dot paper with different colors. Painting is a valuable sensory experience for a child. It provides an opportunity to experiment with color.

Teach your child healthy habits today!

Clean hands can prevent the spread of germs.

Music:

1. **"Brush Your Teeth"** by Raffi.

2. **"My Body"**
   (Sing to the tune of "Where is Thumbkin?")

   This is my body.
   This is my body.
   It's the only one I've got.
   It's the only one I've got.
   I'm going to take good care of it.
   I'm going to take good care of it.
   Yes I am. Yes I am.

Fingerplay:

BRUSHING TEETH

I jiggle the toothbrush again and again.
   (pretend to brush teeth)

I scrub all my teeth for awhile.
I swish the water to rinse them and then
   (puff out cheeks to swish)
I look at myself and I smile.
   (smile at one another)

Science:

Soap Pieces

Add different kinds of soaps and a magnifying glass to the science area. Talk about what each one is used for.

Dramatic Play:

1. **Health Club**

   Mats, fake weights (made from large tinker toys), headbands, and music to represent a health club can be placed in the dramatic play area.

2. **Doctor's Office (Hospital)**

   White clothing, stethoscopes, strip thermometers, magazines, bandages, cots, sheets, and plastic syringes without needles can be placed in the dramatic play area to represent a hospital.

3. **Restaurant**

   Tables, tablecloths, menus, and tablets for taking orders can be placed in the dramatic play area. Paste pictures of food on the menus. A sign for the area could be "Eating for Health."

Arts and Crafts:

1. **Paper Plate Meals**

   Magazines for the children to cut food pictures from the five food groups should be provided. The pictures can be pasted on a paper plate to represent a balanced meal. Plates from microwave dinners, if thoroughly cleaned, work well, too.

2. Body Tracing

Instruct each child to lie on a large piece of paper. Trace the child's body and let him take the tracing home and decorate it with his parents. After this, it can be returned to school for display. This activity should help the children become aware of individual uniqueness and fosters parent-child interaction.

Sensory:

Add shampoo or dish detergent to the sensory table.

Large Muscle:

1. Weight Awareness

The object of this activity is to become aware of weight and to feel the difference between heavy and light. To do this, the child should experiment with body force. Exercise in the following ways: lift arms slowly and gently, stomp on the floor, walk on tiptoes, kick out one leg as hard as possible, very smoothly and lightly slide one foot along the floor. Music can be added to imitate aerobics.

2. Mini-Olympics

Set up various areas for jumping jacks, jogging, relays, and a "beanbag launch." For the "launch" put a beanbag on the top edge of a child's foot and launch it by kicking. Observe the distance each beanbag goes.

Field Trips/Resource People:

1. Take a field trip to:

- hospital
- health care facility
- doctor's office
- dentist's office
- beauty shop
- health club
- drugstore

2. Invite the following resource people to visit the classroom:

- doctor
- nurse
- dentist
- dietician
- aerobics instructor
- beautician

Math:

1. Food Group Sorting

Create a food group display. To do this, encourage the children to bring empty food containers. The food containers can be sorted into food groups. This could be a small group activity or a choice during the self-selected play period.

2. Height and Weight Chart

Weigh and measure each of the children at various times throughout the year. Record the data on a chart. This chart can be posted in the classroom.

Group Time (games, language):

Tasting Party

Prepare for a tasting party. Collect a wide variety of foods. For example, the children could experiment with bananas by dipping them in wheat germ, peanut butter, honey, raisins, etc. To extend this activity, charts can be prepared listing the children's favorite foods.

Cooking:

Fruit Tree Salad

On a plate place a lettuce leaf. On the center of the lettuce, place a pineapple slice. In the hole of the pineapple, place two peeled bananas. Drain 1 small can of fruit cocktail. Spoon the fruit over the bananas.

Multimedia:

The following resources can be found in educational catalogs:

1. Stewart, Georgiana Liccione. *Aerobics for Kids* [record]. Kimbo Educational Records.

2. Johnson, Laura. *Fun Activities for Toddlers* [record]. Kimbo Educational Records.

3. Caesar, Irving. "Songlets for Project Head," *Health-Cleanliness-Safety* [record]. Cleanliness Bureau.

4. *Children's Body Awareness and Movement Exercises* [record]. Stallman Records.

5. *Learning Basic Skills* [25-minute video]. Edu-vid.

6. *The Clean Machine* [video]. Marshfilm.

Books:

The following books can be used to complement the theme:

1. Kalman, Bobbie, & Hughes, Susan. (1986). *The Food We Eat*. New York: Crabtree Publishing Company.

2. Woodruff, Elvira. (1990). *Tubtime*. New York: Holiday House, Inc.

3. Adams, Pam. (1990). *Six in a Bath*. New York: Child's Play International.

4. Berry, Joy. (1987). *Teach Me About Bathtime*. Chicago: Children's Press.

5. Cobb, Vicki. (1989). *Keeping Clean*. New York: Harper Collins Children's Books.

6. McDonnell, Janet. (1990). *Good Health: A Visit from Droopy*. Mankato, MN: Child's World, Inc.

7. Edwards, Frank B., & Bianchi, John. (1990). *Mortimer Mooner Stopped Taking a Bath*. Buffalo, NY: Firefly Books.

8. Hutchins, Pat. (1991). *Tidy Titch*. New York: Greenwillow Books.

9. Moncure, Jane B. (1990). *Caring for My Body*. Mankato, MN: Child's World, Inc.

10. Rockwell, Harlow. (1992). *My Doctor*. New York: Macmillan.

11. Rogers, Alison. (1987). *Luke Has Asthma*. Burlington, VT: Waterfront Books.

12. Scott, Ann Herbert. (1992). *On Mother's Lap*. Boston: Houghton Mifflin.

13. Cowen-Fletcher, Jane. (1993). *Mama Zooms*. New York: Scholastic Inc.

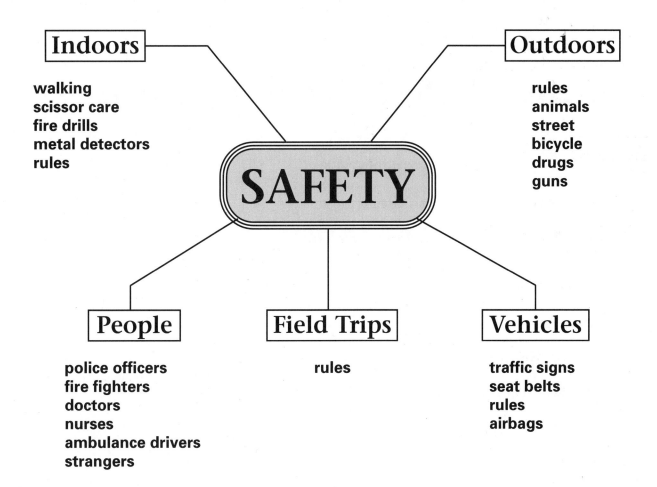

Indoors

walking
scissor care
fire drills
metal detectors
rules

Outdoors

rules
animals
street
bicycle
drugs
guns

SAFETY

People

police officers
fire fighters
doctors
nurses
ambulance drivers
strangers

Field Trips

rules

Vehicles

traffic signs
seat belts
rules
airbags

Theme Goals:

Through participating in the experiences provided by this theme, the children may learn:

1. Indoor safety precautions.

2. Play yard safety.

3. People who keep us safe.

4. Field trip safety.

5. Vehicle safety.

Concepts for the Children to Learn:

1. We walk indoors.

2. Play yard rules help keep us safe.

3. We have special rules for field trips.

4. Fire drills prepare us for emergencies.

5. Scissors need to be handled carefully.

6. Wearing a seat belt is practicing car safety.

7. Traffic signs help prevent accidents.

8. Police officers, fire fighters, doctors, nurses, and ambulance drivers help keep us safe.

9. Only talk to people you know.

Vocabulary:

1. **safety**—freedom from danger.

2. **sign**—a lettered board.

3. **seat belt**—strap that holds a person in a vehicle.

4. **rule**—the way we are to act.

5. **fire drill**—practicing leaving the building in case of a fire.

Bulletin Board

The purpose of this bulletin board is to call attention to safety signs. The children are to match the safety sign with its outline on the board. To prepare this bulletin board, construct six safety signs out of tagboard, each a different shape. Color appropriately and laminate. Trace the outline of these signs onto black construction paper to create shadow signs as illustrated. Staple the shadow signs to the bulletin board. Punch holes in the safety signs using a hole punch. The children can match the shape of the safety signs to the shadow signs by hanging them on the appropriate push pins.

Parent Letter

Dear Parents,

Safety will be the focus of our next unit. We will be learning about safety at school, at home, and outdoors. Through this unit the children will also become more aware of traffic signs and their importance.

At School

A few of the activities planned for this unit include:

- taking a safety walk to practice crossing streets.
- counting the number of traffic signs that are in our school neighborhood.
- visiting the fire station on Tuesday morning. We will be leaving at 9:30 A.M. and should return to school by 11:00 A.M.

At Home

One of the songs we will be learning follows. It will help your child become aware of the purpose and colors of a traffic light. You may enjoy singing the song at home with your child. The song is sung to the tune of "Twinkle, Twinkle, Little Star." The words are as follows:

> Twinkle, twinkle, traffic light,
> Standing on the corner bright.
> When it's green it's time to go.
> When it's red it's stop, you know.
> Twinkle, twinkle, traffic light,
> Standing on the corner bright.

During your daily routines, share safety tips with your child.

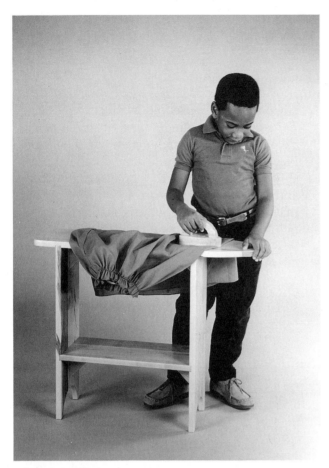

Safety in even the simplest activities must be reinforced.

Music:

1. **"Twinkle, Twinkle, Traffic Light"**
   (Sing to the tune of "Twinkle, Twinkle, Little Star")

   Twinkle, twinkle, traffic light,
   Standing on the corner bright.
   When it's green it's time to go.
   When its red it's stop, you know.
   Twinkle, twinkle, traffic light,
   Standing on the corner bright.

2. **"Do You Know the Police Officer"**
   (Sing to the tune of "The Muffin Man")

   Oh, do you know the police officer,
   The police officer, the police officer?
   Oh, do you know the police officer
   Who helps me cross the street?

This song can be extended. For example, the song can be continued substituting "who helps me when I'm lost" or "who helps one cross the street."

3. **"We Are Safe"**
   (Sing to the tune of "Mulberry Bush")

   This is the way that we are safe
   We are safe, we are safe.
   This is the way that we are safe
   Every day of the year.

   This is the way we cross the street—
   Look left, then right, left then right.
   This is the way we cross the street—

   Look left, then right for safety.
   This is the way we ride in the car—
   Sit up straight, buckle your belt.
   This is the way we ride in the car—
   Buckle your belt for safety.

   Resource: Wilmes, Liz & Dick. (1983). *Everyday Circle Times*. Illinois: Building Blocks Publishing.

Fingerplays:

SILLY TEDDY BEAR

Silly little teddy bear
Stood up in a rocking chair.
   (make rocking movement)
Now he has to stay in bed
   (lay head on hands)
With a bandage round his head.
   (circular movement of hand around head)

CROSSING STREETS

At the curb before I cross
I stop my running feet
   (point to feet)
And look both ways to left and right
   (look left and right)
Before I cross the street.
Lest autos running quietly
Might come as a surprise.
I just don't listen with my ears
   (point to ears)
But look with both my eyes.
   (point to eyes)

RED LIGHT

Red light, red light what do you say?
I say, "Stop and stop right away!"
   (hold palms of both hands up)
Yellow light, yellow light what do you say?
I say, "Wait till the light turns green."
   (hold one palm of hand up)
Green light, green light what do you say?
I say "Go, but look each way."
   (circle arm in forward motion and turn head
   to the right and left)
Thank you, thank you, red, yellow, green
Now I know what the traffic light means.

FIVE POLICE OFFICERS

Five strong police officers standing by a store.
   (hold up the one hand)
One became a traffic cop, then there were four.
   (hold up four fingers)
Four strong police officers watching over me.
One took a lost boy home, then there were
three.
   (hold up three fingers)
Three strong police officers all dressed in blue.
One stopped a speeding car and then there
were two.
   (hold up two fingers)
Two strong police officers, how fast they can
run.
One caught a bad man and then there was one.
   (hold up one finger)
One strong police officer saw some smoke one
day.
He called a fire fighter who put it out right
away.

THE CROSSING GUARD

The crossing guard keeps us safe
As he works from day to day.
He holds the stop sign high in the air.
   (hold palm of hand up)
For the traffic to obey.
And when the cars have completely stopped
And its as safe as can be,
He signals us to walk across
   (make a beckoning motion)
The street very carefully.

Science:

1. **Sorting for Safety**

   Collect empty household product containers.
   Include safe and dangerous items such as
   cleaning supplies, orange juice containers, etc.
   Place all the items in one large box. The
   children can separate the containers into "safe"
   and "dangerous" categories. Younger children
   may be ableto separate the containers into
   edible and nonedible categories.

2. **All About Me**

   On a table place identification items. Prepare a
   separate card for each child. Record the
   following information on the cards:

   - height
   - weight
   - color hair
   - color eyes
   - fingerprint
   - signature (if child can or a teacher can help)

Dramatic Play:

1. **Fire Engine**

   A large cardboard box can be decorated by the
   children as a fire engine with yellow or red
   tempera paint. When the fire engine is dry,
   place it in the dramatic play area with short
   hoses and fire fighter hats. This prop could
   also be placed outdoors, weather permitting.

2. **Prop Boxes**

   Develop prop boxes such as:

   Fire Fighter
   bell
   jacket/uniform
   boots
   whistle
   hose
   oxygen mask
   hat

   Police Officer
   hat
   badges

handcuffs
stop sign (for holding)

3. **Fire Fighter Jackets**

Construct fire fighter jackets out of large paper bags. Begin by cutting three holes. One hole is used for the child's head at the top of the bag. Then cut two large holes for arms. These props may encourage the children to dramatize the roles of the fire fighters.

4. **Seat Belts**

Collect child-sized car seats. Place them around like chairs, letting the children adjust them for themselves or their dolls.

Arts and Crafts:

1. **Fire Fighter Hats**

Cut fire fighter hats out of large sheets of red construction paper for the children to wear.

2. **Easel Painting**

On the easel, place cut-out shapes of fire hats or boots.

3. **Traffic Lights**

Construct stop and go lights out of shoeboxes. Tape the lid to the bottom of the box. Cover with black construction paper and have children place green, yellow, and red circles in correct order on the box. The red circle should be placed on the top, yellow in the middle, and green on the bottom.

4. **Officer Hats and Badges**

Police officer hats and badges can be constructed out of paper and colored with crayons or felt-tip watercolor markers.

Sensory:

1. **Pumps and Hoses**

Water pumps, hoses, and water can be placed in the sensory table.

2. **Trucks**

Small toy fire trucks and police cars can be placed in the sensory table with sand.

Large Muscle:

1. **Safety Walk**

Take a safety walk. Practice observing traffic lights when crossing the street. Point out special hazards to the children.

2. **Stop, Drop, and Roll**

Practice "Stop, Drop, and Roll" with the children. This will be valuable to them if they are ever involved in a fire and their clothes happen to catch on fire. Usually a fire fighter will teach them this technique while visiting the fire station.

Field Trips/Resource People:

1. **Fire Fighter**

Invite a fire fighter to the classroom. Ask him to bring fire fighter clothing and equipment and to discuss each item.

2. **Police Car**

Invite a police officer to visit the classroom. Ask him to bring a police car to show the children.

Math:

1. **Sequencing Hats**

Draw pictures of three police hats. Make each picture identical except design three different sizes. The children can sequence the objects from largest to smallest or smallest to largest. Discuss the sizes and ask which is largest, smallest, middle.

2. **Safety Items**

Walk around the school and observe the number of safety items. Included may be exit signs, fire drill posters, fire extinguishers, sprinkler systems, fire alarm/drill bells, etc.

Social Studies:

1. **Safety Pictures and Signs**

   Post safety pictures and signs around the room.

2. **Stop and Go Light**

   Draw a large stop and go light on a piece of tagboard. Color with felt-tip markers. Print the following across from the corresponding colors:

   Green means go we all know
   Yellow means wait even if you're late,
   Red means stop!

3. **Safety Signs**

   Take a walk and watch for safety signs. Discuss the colors and letters on each sign.

Group Time (games, language):

Toy Safety

Collect a variety of unsafe toys that may have sharp edges, a broken wagon, etc. During group time discuss the dangers of each toy.

Cooking:

1. **Banana Rounds**

   4 medium bananas
   1/2 tablespoon honey
   1/8 teaspoon nutmeg
   1/8 teaspoon cinnamon
   1/4 cup wheat germ

   The children can peel the bananas and then slice them with a plastic knife. Measure the spices, wheat germ, and honey. Finally, mix them with the bananas. Chill. Serves 8.

2. **Stop Signs**

   eight-sided crackers
   peanut butter
   jelly

   Spread a thin layer of peanut butter and jelly on each cracker.

3. **Yield Signs**

   triangle crackers
   yellow cheese

   Cut yellow cheese into triangles. Put the cheese on the crackers.

Multimedia:

The following resources are available through educational catalogs:

1. *Learning Basic Skills Through Music, Health and Safety* [record]. Freeport, NY: Activity Records, Inc.

2. Poelker, Kathy Lencinski. "Fire Station," *Look at My World Record* [record].

3. Moore, Thomas. *Safe Not Sorry* [record].

4. *Bean Bag Activities & Coordination Skills* [record]. Kimbo Records.

Books:

The following books can be used to complement the theme:

1. Hoban, Tana. (1987). *I Read Signs*. New York: Morrow.

2. Chacon, Rick. (1985). *You Can Say "No!"* Huntington Beach, CA: Teacher Created Materials, Inc.

3. Chlad, Dorothy. (1987). *Playing on the Playground*. Chicago: Children's Press.

4. Molnar, Dorothy E., & Fenton, Stephen H. (1991). *Who Will Pick Me Up When I Fall?* Morton Grove, IL: Albert Whitman.

5. Patz, Nancy. (1990). *No Thumping No Bumping No Rumpus Tonight!* New York: Macmillan.

6. Wilson, Sarah. (1988). *Beware the Dragon!* New York: Harper Collins.

7. Chlad, Dorothy. (1992). *Bicycles Are Fun to Ride*. Chicago: Children's Press.

8. Crary, Elizabeth. (1985). *I'm Lost*. Seattle, WA: Parenting Press.

9. Klingel, Cynthia F. (1986). *Safety First-School*. Mankato, MN: Creative Education, Inc.

10. Reihecky, Janet. (1990). *Carefulness*. Mankato, MN: Child World, Inc.

11. Perry, Kate. (1992). *Mr. Toad to the Rescue*. Hauppauge, NY: Barron's Educational Series, Inc.

APPENDIX A

INTERNATIONAL HOLIDAYS

When planning the curriculum, it is important to note international holidays. The exact date of the holiday may vary from year to year; consequently, it is important to check with parents or a reference librarian at a local library. These international holidays for Christians, Buddhists, Eastern Orthodox, Hindus, Jews, and Muslims are as follows:

Christian

Ash Wednesday
Palm Sunday—the Sunday before Easter, which commemorates the triumphant entry of Jesus in Jerusalem.
Holy Thursday—also known as Maundy Thursday; it is the Thursday of Holy Week.
Good Friday—commemorates the crucifixion of Jesus.
Easter—celebrates the resurrection of Jesus.
Christmas Eve
Christmas Day—commemorates the birth of Jesus.

Buddhist

Nirvana Day (Mahayana Sect)—observes the passing of Sakyamuni into Nirvana. He obtained enlightenment and became a Buddha.
Magna Puja (Theravada Sect)—one of the holiest Buddhist holidays; it marks the occasion when 1,250 of Buddha's disciples gathered spontaneously to hear him speak.
Buddha Day (Mahayana Sect)—this service commemorates the birth of Gautama in Lumbini Garden. Amida, the Buddha of Infinite Wisdom and Compassion, manifested himself among men in the person Gautama.
Versakha Piya (Theravada Sect)—the most sacred of the Buddhist days. It celebrates the birth, death, and enlightenment of Buddha.
Maharram—marks the beginning of Buddhist Lent, it is the anniversary of Buddha's sermon to the first five disciples.
Vassana (Theravada Sect)—the beginning of the three-month period when monks stay in their temple to study and meditate.
Bon (Mahayana Sect)—an occasion for rejoicing in the enlightenment offered by the Buddha; often referred to as a "Gathering of Joy." Buddha had saved the life of the mother Moggallana. The day is in remembrance of all those who have passed away.
Pavarana (Theravada Sect)—celebrates Buddha's return to earth after spending one Lent season preaching in heaven.
Bodhi Day (Mahayana Sect)—celebrates the enlightenment of Buddha.

Eastern Orthodox

Christmas
First Day of Lent—begins a period of fasting and penitence in preparation for Easter.
Easter Sunday—celebrates the resurrection of Jesus.
Ascension Day—the 40th day after Easter, commemorates the ascension of Jesus to heaven.
Pentecost—commemorates the descent of the Holy Spirit upon the Apostles, 50 days after Easter Sunday. Marks the beginning of the Christian Church.

Hindu

Pongal Sankrandi—a three-day harvest festival.

Vasanta Pachami—celebrated in honor of Saraswati, the charming and sophisticated goddess of scholars.

Shivarari—a solemn festival devoted to the worship of Shiva, the most powerful of deities of the Hindu pantheon.

Holi—celebrates the advent of spring.

Ganguar—celebrated in honor of Parvari, the consort of Lord Shiva.

Ram Navami—birthday of the God Rama.

Hanuman Jayanti—birthday of Monkey God Humumanji.

Meenakshi Kalyanam—the annual commemoration of the marriage of Meenakshi to Lord Shiva.

Teej—celebrates the arrival of the monsoon; Parvari is the presiding deity.

Jewish

Yom Kippur—the most holy day of the Jewish year, it is marked by fasting and prayer as Jews seek forgiveness from God and man.

Sukkot—commemorates the 40-year wandering of Israelites in the desert on the way to the Promised Land; expresses thanksgiving for the fall harvest.

Simchat Torah—celebrates the conclusion of the public reading of the Pentateuch and its beginning anew, thus affirming that the study of God's word is an unending process. Concludes the Sukkot Festival.

Hanukkah—the eight-day festival that celebrates the rededication of the Temple to the service of God. Commemorates the Maccabean victory over Antiochus, who sought to suppress freedom of worship.

Purim—marks the salvation of the Jews of ancient Persia through the intervention of Queen Esther, from Haman's plot to exterminate them.

Passover—an eight-day festival marking ancient Israel's deliverance from Egyptian bondage.

Yom Hashoah—day of remembrance for victims of Nazi Holocaust.

Sahvout—celebrates the covenant established at Sinai between God and Israel and the revelation of the Ten Commandments.

Rosh Hashanah—the first of the High Holy Days marking the beginning of a ten-day period of penitence and spiritual renewal.

Muslim

Isra and Miraj—commemorates the anniversary of the night journey of the Prophet and his ascension to heaven.

Ramadan—the beginning of the month of fasting from sunrise to sunset.

Id al-Fitr—end of the month of fasting from sunrise to sunset; first day of pilgrimage to Mecca.

Hajj—the first day of pilgrimage to Mecca.

Day of Amfat—gathering of the pilgrims.

Id al-adha—commemorates the Feast of the Sacrifice.

Muharram—the Muslim New Year; marks the beginning of the Hedjra Year 1412.

Id al-Mawlid—commemorates the nativity and death of Prophet Muhammad and his flight from Mecca to Medina.

APPENDIX B

EARLY CHILDHOOD COMMERCIAL SUPPLIERS

ABC School Supply, Inc.
3312 N. Berkeley Lake Road
Delouth, Georgia 30136
(770) 497-0001

American Guidance Service
Publisher's Building
Circle Pines, Minnesota 55014
(612) 786-4343

Beckley Cardy
One East First Street
Duluth, Minnesota 55802
1-800-227-1178

Childcraft Educational Corporation
P.O. Box 3239
Lancaster, Pennsylvania 17604

Children's Press
5440 North Cumberland Avenue
Chicago, Illinois 60656
1-800-621-1115

Classic School Products
174 Semoran Commerce Place, Suite A106
Apopka, Florida 32703
1-800-394-9661

Community Playthings
Route 213
Rifton, New York 12471
(914) 658-8351

Constructive Playthings
1227 East 119th Street
Grandview, Missouri 64030-1117
1-800-832-0224

Cuisenaire Company of America, Inc.
12 Church Street, Box D
New Rochelle, New York 10802
1-800-237-3142

Delmar Publishers
3 Columbia Circle
Box 15-015
Albany, New York 12212-5015
1-800-998-7498

Didax Educational Resources
395 Main Sreet
Rowley, Massachusetts 01969
(508) 948-2340

Environments, Inc.
P.O. Box 1348
Beaufort, South Carolina 29901-1348
(803) 846-8155

Gryphon House, Inc.
3706 Otis Street
Mt. Rainier, Maryland 20712

The Highsmith Co., Inc.
W5527 Highway 106
P.O. Box 800
Fort Atkinson, Wisconsin 53538-0800
1-800-558-2110

J. L. Hammett
P.O. Box 9057
Braintree, Massachusetts 02184-9704
1-800-333-4600

Judy/Instructo
4325 Hiawatha Avenue
Minneapolis, Minnesota 55406

Kaplan School Supply Corporation
P.O. Box 609
Lewisville, North Carolina 27023-0609
1-800-334-2014

Kentucky School Supply
Dept. 21
P.O. Box 886
Elizabethtown, Kentucky 42702
1-800-626-4405

Kimbo Educational
10 North Third Avenue
Long Branch, New Jersey 07740
1-800-631-2187

Lakeshore Learning Materials
2695 E. Dominguez Street
Carson, California 90749
1-800-421-5354

Latta's School and Office Supplies
P.O. Box 128
2218 Main Street
Cedar Falls, Iowa 50613
(319) 266-3501

Nasco
901 Janesville Avenue
Fort Atkinson, Wisconsin 53538
1-800-558-9595

Primary Educator
1200 Keystone Avenue
P.O. Box 24155
Lansing, Michigan 48909-4155
1-800-444-1773

Redleaf Press
450 North Syndicate
Suite 5
St. Paul, Minnesota 55104-4125
(612) 641-6629

St. Paul Book and Stationery
1233 West County Road E
St. Paul, Minnesota 55112
1-800-338-SPBS (7727)

Valley School Supply
1000 North Bluemound Drive
P.O. Box 1579
Appleton, Wisconsin 54913
1-800-242-3433

Warren's Educational Supplies
980 West San Bernardino Road
Covina, California 91722-4196
(818) 966-1731

RAINY DAY ACTIVITIES*

1. Get Acquainted Game

The children sit in a circle formation. The teacher begins the game by saying, "My name is ——— and I'm going to roll the ball to ———." Continue playing the game until every child has a turn. A variation of the game is have the children stand in a circle and bounce the ball to each other. This game is a fun way for the children to learn each other's names.

2. Hide the Ball

Choose several children and ask them to cover their eyes. Then hide a small ball, or other object, in an observable place. Ask the children to uncover their eyes and try to find the ball. The first child to find the ball hides it again.

3. "Which Ball is Gone?"

In the center of the circle, place six colored balls, cubes, beads, shapes, etc., in a row. Ask a child to close his eyes. Then ask another child to remove one of the objects and hide it behind him. The first child uncovers his eyes and tells which colored object is missing from the row. The game continues until all the selections have been made. When using with older children, two objects may be removed at a time to further challenge their abilities.

4. "What Sound is That?"

The purpose of this game is to promote the development of listening skills. Begin by asking the children to close their eyes. Make a familiar sound. Then ask a child to identify it. Sources of sound may include:

tearing paper	blowing a pitch pipe	raising or lowering
sharpening a pencil	dropping an object	window shades
walking, running,	moving a desk or	leafing through
shuffling feet	chair	book pages
clapping hands	snapping fingers	cutting with
sneezing, coughing	blowing nose	scissors
tapping on glass,	opening or closing	snapping rubber
wood, or metal	drawer	bands
jingling money	stirring paint in	ringing a bell
opening a window	a jar	clicking the tongue
pouring water	clearing the throat	crumpling paper
shuffling cards	splashing water	opening a box
blowing a whistle	rubbing sandpaper	sighing
banging blocks	together	stamping feet
bouncing ball	chattering teeth	rubbing palms
shaking a rattle	sweeping sound,	together
turning the lights on	such as a brush or	rattling keys
knocking on a door	broom	

A variation of this game could be played by having a child make a sound. Then the other children and the teacher close their eyes and attempt to identify the sound. For older children this game can be varied with the production of two sounds. Begin by asking the children if the sounds are the same or different. Then have them identify the sounds.

5. "Near or Far?"

The purpose of this game is to locate sound. First, tell the children to close their eyes. Then play a sound recorded on a cassette tape. Ask the children to identify the sound as being near or far away.

6. Descriptions

The purpose of this game is to encourage expressive language skills. Begin by asking each child to describe himself. Included with the description can be the color of his eyes, hair, and clothing. The teacher might prefer to use an imaginative introduction such as: "One by one, you may take turns sitting up here in Alfred's magic chair and describe yourself to Alfred." Another approach may be to say, "Pretend that you must meet somebody at a very crowded airport who has never seen you before. How would you describe yourself so that the person would be sure to know who you are?"

A variation for older children would be to have one of the children describe another child without revealing the name of the person he is describing. To illustrate, the teacher might say, "I'm thinking of someone with shiny red hair, blue eyes, many freckles, etc...." The child being described should stand up.

7. Mirrored Movements

The purpose of this game is to encourage awareness of body parts through mirrored movements. Begin the activity by making movements. Encourage the children to mirror your movements. After the children understand the game, they may individually take the leader role.

8. Little Red Wagon Painted Red

As a prop for the game, cut a red wagon with wheels out of construction paper. Then cut rectangles the same size as the box of the red wagon. Include purple, blue, yellow, green, orange, brown, black, and pink colors.

Sing the song to the tune of **"Skip to My Lou."**

*Little red wagon painted **red.***
*Little red wagon painted **red.***
*Little red wagon painted **red.***
What color would it be?

Give each child a turn to pick and name a color. As the song is sung, let the child change the wagon color.

9. Police Officer Game

Select one child to be the police officer. Ask him to find a lost child. Describe one of the children in the circle. The child who is the police officer will use the description as a clue to find the "missing child."

10. Mother Cat and Baby Kits

Choose one child to be the mother cat. Then ask the mother cat to go to sleep in the center of the circle, covering his eyes. Then choose several children to be kittens. The verse below is chanted as the baby kittens hide in different parts of the classroom. Following this, the mother cat hunts for them. When all of the kittens have been located, another mother cat may be selected. The number of times the game is repeated depends upon the children's interest and attention span.

Mother cat lies fast asleep.

To her side the kittens creep.

But the kittens like to play.

Softly now they creep away.

Mother cat wakes up to see.

No little kittens. Where can they be?

11. Memory Game

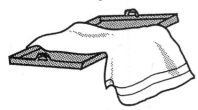

Collect common household items, a towel, and tray. Place the items on the tray. Show the tray containing the items. Cover with a towel. Then ask the children to recall the names of the items on the tray. To ensure success, begin the activity with only two or three objects for young children. Additional objects can be added depending upon the developmental maturity of the children.

12. Cobbler, Mend My Shoes

Sit the children in a circle formation. Then select one child to sit in the center. This child gives a shoe to a child in the circle, and then closes his eyes. The children in the circle pass the shoe around behind them while the rhyme is chanted. When the chant is finished, the shoe is no longer passed. The last child with the shoe in his hand holds the shoe behind his back. Then the child sitting in the center tries to guess who has the shoe.

Cobbler, cobbler, mend my shoe

Have it done by half past two

Stitch it up and stitch it down

Now see with whom the shoe is found.

13. Huckle Buckle Beanstalk

Ask the children to sit in a circle. Once seated, tell them to close their eyes. Then hide a small ball in an obvious place. Say, "Ready." Encourage all of the children to hunt for the object. Each child who spots it returns to a place in the circle and says, "Huckle buckle beanstalk." No one must tell where he has seen the ball until all the children have seen it.

14. What's Different?

Sit all of the children in a circle formation. Ask one child to sit in the center. The rest of the children are told to look closely at the child sitting in the center. Then the children are told to cover their eyes while you change some detail on the child in the center. For example, you may place a hat on the child, untie his shoe, remove a shoe, roll up one sleeve, etc. The children sitting in the circle act as detective to determine "what's different?"

15. Cookie Jar

Sit the children in a circle formation on the floor with their legs crossed. Together they repeat a rhythmic chant while using alternating leg-hand clap to emphasize the rhythm. The chant is as follows.

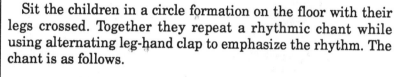

Someone took the cookies from the cookie jar.

Who took the cookies from the cookie jar?

Mary took the cookies from the cookie jar.

Mary took the cookies from the cookie jar?

Who, me? (Mary)

Yes, you. (all children)

Couldn't be. (Mary)

Then who? (all children)

——— *took the cookies from the cookie jar.* (Mary names another child.)

Use each child's name.

16. Hide and Seek Tonal Matching

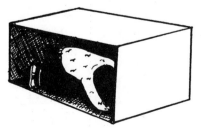

Sit the children in a circle formation. Ask one child to hide in the room while the other children cover their eyes. The children in the circle sing, "Where is ——— hiding?" The child who is hiding responds by singing back, "Here I am." With their eyes remaining closed, the children point in the direction of the hiding child. All open eyes and the child emerges from his hiding place.

17. Listening and Naming

This game is most successful with a small group of children. The children should take turns shutting their eyes and identifying sounds as you tap with a wooden dowel on an object such as glass, triangle, drum, wooden block, cardboard box, rubber ball, etc.

18. Funny Shapes

Ask each child to choose a partner. One partner must make a large shape with his body. The other partner must follow the directions of movement. Roles reverse for the second set of directions. Provide directions such as:

1. Make a big shape.

go *over*
go *under*
go *through*
go *around*

2. Make a small shape.

go *over*
go *under*
go *through*
go *around*

19. Drop the Handkerchief

Direct the children to stand in a circle formation. Ask one child to run around the outside of the circle, dropping a handkerchief behind another child. The child who has the handkerchief dropped behind him must pick it up and chase the child who dropped it. The first child tries to return to the vacated space by running before he is tagged.

20. "If You Please"

This game is a simple variation of "Simon Says." Ask the children to form a circle around a leader who gives directions, some of which are prefaced with "if you please." The children are to follow only the "if you please" directions, ignoring any that do not begin with "if you please." Directions to be used may include walking forward, hopping on one foot, bending forward, standing tall, etc. This game can be varied by having the children follow the directions when the leader says, "do this," and not when he says, "do that." Play only one version of this game on a single day. Too much variety will confuse the children.

194

21. Duck Duck Goose

Ask the children to squat in a circle formation. Then ask one child to walk around the outside of circle, lightly touching each child's head and saying "Duck, Duck." When he touches another child and says "Goose," that child chases him around the circle. If the child who was "it" returns to the "goose's" place without being tagged, he remains. When this happens, the tapped child is "it." This game is appropriate for older four-, five-, six-, and seven-year-old children.

22. Fruit Basket Upset

Ask the children to sit in a circle formation on chairs or on carpet squares. Then ask one child to sit in the middle of the circle as the chef. Hand pictures of various fruits to the rest of the children. Then to continue the game, ask the chef to call out the name of a fruit. The children holding that particular fruit exchange places. If the chef calls out, "fruit basket upset," all of the children must exchange places, including the chef. The child who doesn't find a place is the new chef. A variation of this game would be bread basket upset. For this game use pictures of breads, rolls, bagels, muffins, breadsticks, etc. This game is appropriate for older children.

23. Bear Hunt

This is a rhythmic chant which may easily be varied. Start by chanting each line, encouraging the children to repeat the line.

Teacher: *Let's go on a bear hunt.*

Children: *(Repeat. Imitate walk by slapping knees alternately.)*

Teacher:
I see a wheat field.
Can't go over it;
Can't go under it.
Let's go through it.
(arms straight ahead like you're parting wheat)

I see a bridge.
Can't go over it;
Can't go under it.
Let's swim.
(arms in swimming motion)

I see a tree.
Can't go over it;
Can't go under it.
Let's go up it.
(climb and look)

I see a swamp.
Can't go over it;
Can't go under it.
Let's go through it.
(pull hands up and down slowly)

I see a cave.
Can't go over it;
Can't go under it.
Let's go in.
(walking motion)

I see two eyes. I see two ears.
I see a nose. I see a mouth.
It's a BEAR!!!
(Do all in reverse very fast)

24. "Guess Who?"

Individually tape the children's voices. Play the tape during group time, and let the children identify their classmates' voices.

25. Shadow Fun

Hang a bed sheet up in the classroom for use as a projection screen. Then place a light source such as a slide, filmstrip, or overhead projector a few feet behind the screen. Ask two of the children to stand behind the sheet. Then encourage one of the two children to walk in front of the projector light. When this happens, the children are to give the name of the person who is moving.

26. If This Is Red— Nod Your Head

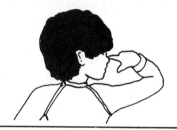

Point to an object in the room and say, "If this is green, shake your hand. If this is yellow, touch your nose." If the object is not the color stated, children should not imitate the requested action.

27. Freeze

Encourage the children to imitate activities such as washing dishes, cleaning house, dancing, etc. Approximately every 10 to 20 seconds, call out "Freeze!" When this occurs, the children are to stop whatever they are doing and remain frozen until you say, "Thaw" or "Move." A variation of this activity would be to use music. When the music stops, the children freeze their movements.

28. Spy the Object

Designate a large area on the floor as home base. Then select an object and show it to the children. Ask the children to cover their eyes while you place the object in an observable place in the room. Then encourage the children to open their eyes and search for the object. As each child spies the object he quietly returns to the home base area without telling. The other children continue searching until all have found the object. After all the children are seated, they may share where the object is placed.

29. Who Is Gone?

This game is played in a circle format. Begin by asking a child to close his eyes. Then point to a child to leave the circle and go to a spot where he can't be seen. The child with his eyes closed opens them at your word, then looks around the circle and identifies the friend who is missing.

30. It's Me

Seat the children in a circle formation, and place a chair in the center. Choose one child to sit on a chair in the circle, closing his eyes. After this, ask another child to walk up softly behind the chair and tap the child on the shoulder. The seated child asks, "Who is tapping?" The other child replies, "It's me." By listening to the response, the seated child identifies the other child.

31. Feeling and Naming

Ask a child to stand with his back to you, placing his hands behind him. Then place an object in the child's hands for identification by feeling it. Nature materials can be used such as leaves, shells, fruit, etc. A ball, doll, block, Lego piece, puzzle piece, crayon, etc., may also be used.

32. Doggy, Doggy, Where's Your Bone?

Sit the children in a circle formation. Then place a chair in the center of the circle. Place a block under the chair. Select one child, the dog, to sit on the chair and close his eyes. Then point to another child. This child must try to get the dog's bone from under the chair without making a noise. After the child returns to his place in the circle, all the children place their hands behind them. Then in unison the children say, "Doggy, Doggy, where's your bone?" During the game, each dog has three guesses as to who has the bone.

Index by Subject

200

The Essentials of Early Education

Carol Gestwicki, M.A.

Central Piedmont Community College, North Carolina

Young children need people with specific knowledge, skills, and attitudes, who have thoughtfully prepared to enter into caring relationships with young children and their families. This book examines the world of early education and assists in the process of professional growth for those who are interested in considering it as their future. Designed to be the ideal motivational tool for beginning teachers entering the field, The Essentials of Early Education encourages students to be active participants in the decision making process of becoming early childhood teachers. All the phases of early childhood education are thoroughly covered: the scope of children served, the types of programs, different styles and philosophies of teaching, in addition to defining all the aspects of a quality education and the teacher's role in education today.

FEATURES:

- Written in brief, interactive style that is career focused.
- Full color art program.
- "Theory into Practice" section in each chapter introduces real teachers and issues.
- Supported with multiple classroom activities and quizzes to enhance analytical and critical thinking skills.
- Unique "Time Line of ECE" feature runs as a footnote throughout the text with an event or person and its relevance to early childhood or development.
- A running glossary appears in the column so that students have all the information they need to know at their fingertips.

TABLE OF CONTENTS:

THE STARTING POINT. Decision Making. Early Childhood Education Today. What Quality Early Education Looks Like. What Teachers Do. DEVELOPING AS A TEACHER. Why Become a Teacher? Growing Oneself as a Teacher. Challenges for Early Educators. THE PROFESSION COMES OF AGE. Roots of Early Education. The Modern Profession. Professional Education & Career Directions. Current Issues in Early Education. The Road Ahead.

355 pp., softcover, 8" x 10"
Text 0-8273-7282-5
Instructor's Manual 0-8273-7283-3

To Order Call Toll Free
1-800-354-9706
Fax: 1-800-487-8488
or use the Order Form on the
last page of this book.

Health, Safety & Nutrition for the Young Child, 4E

Lynn R. Marotz, Ph.D., University of Kansas
Marie Z. Cross, Ph.D., University of Kansas
Jeanettia M. Rush, R.D., M.A.

We are pleased to present the fourth edition of the best selling textbook in early education. This full color book sets
the standard for the three most crucial areas of child development: children's health status, a safe, yet challenging
learning environment and proper nutrition. The new edition includes updated information on the most current
issues in child care. Emphasis is given to the topic of
quality child care and organizing quality care environments for children. This edition includes increased cov-
erage of AIDS and children, Attention Deficit Disorder
(ADD), ADHD, Sudden Infant Death Syndrome (SIDS),
lead poisoning, diabetes, seizures, allergies, asthma, eczema, sickle cell anemia,
immunization, emergency care, and common illnesses as
well as life threatening conditions.

FEATURES:
- Full color illustrations and photographs bring theory and practice alive!
- Key words are noted in color, italicized, and defined in the glossary (reinforcing the students'
  analytical and critical thinking skills).
- Each chapter contain summaries, hands-on learning activities and review questions to foster
  active learning skills
- Electronic study guide, packaged with text, includes answers to review questions, test items,
  resources and discussion topics.

WHAT'S NEW
- The new "Food Guide Pyramid"
- Toddler feeding
- Optional electronic study guide
- Infant feeding concerns
- Sample activity plans

TABLE OF CONTENTS:
HEALTH, SAFETY, & NUTRITION: AN INTRODUCTION: Interrelationship of Health, Safety, &
Nutrition. HEALTH OF THE YOUNG CHILD: MAXIMIZING THE CHILD'S POTENTIAL:
Promoting Good Health. Health Appraisals. Health Assessment Tools. Conditions Affecting
Children's Health. The Infectious Process & Effective Control. Communicable & Acute Illness:
Identification & Management, SAFETY FOR THE YOUNG CHILD: Creating a Safe Environment.
Safety Management. Management of Accidents & Injuries. Child Abuse & Neglect. Educational
Experience for Young Children. FOODS & NUTRIENTS: BASIC CONCEPTS: Nutritional
Guidelines. Nutrients That Provide Energy. Nutrients That Promote Growth of Body Tissues.
Nutrients That Regulate Body Functions. NUTRITION & THE YOUNG CHILD. Infant Feeding.
Feeding the Toddler & the Preschool Child. Planning & Serving Nutritious Meals. Food Safety &
Economy. Nutrition Education Concepts & Activities. APPENDICES: Nutrition Analysis of
Various Fast Foods. Growth Charts for Boys & Girls. Sources of Free & Inexpensive Materials
Related to Health, Safety, & Nutrition. Federal Food Program. Glossary. Index.

506 pp., softcover, 7 3/8" x 9 1/4"
Text 0-8273-8353-3   Instructor's Guide 0-8273-7274-4

Flash!

Seeing Young Children: A Guide to Observing and Recording Behavior, 3E

Warren R. Bentzen, Ph.D.
State University of New York at Plattsburgh

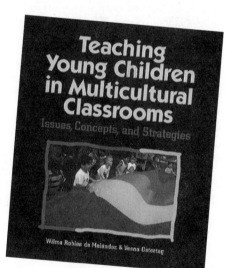

Seeing Young Children provides the essential guidelines for observing young children. This text includes the steps one must take before entering the observation setting to professional ethics and confidentiality.

TABLE OF CONTENTS:
OVERVIEW: Introduction. Overview of Developmental Theories. General Guidelines for Observing Children. THE ELEMENTS OF OBSERVATION: Methods, Behaviors, Plans, and Contexts. An Introduction to Observation & Recording Methods. Narrative Descriptions. Time Sampling. Event Sampling. Diary Description. Anecdotal Records. Frequency Counts or Duration Records. Checklists. Application: Recording Methods in Action. Interpretations of Observations, Implementation of Findings, and Ongoing Evaluation. OBSERVATION EXERCISES: Introduction & Preparation. Observing the Newborn: Birth to One Month. Observing the Infant (One to Twenty-Four Months). The Young Child: Ages Two Through Five. MIDDLE CHILDHOOD: The School-Age Years. Introduction & Preparation. The School-Age Years: The Six-Year Old Child. The School-Age Years: The Seven- and Eight-Year Old Child.

384pp., softcover, 7 3/8" x 9 1/4"
Text 0-8273-7665-0
Instructor's Manual 0-8273-7666-9

Teaching Young Children in Multicultural Classrooms

Wilma Robles DeMelendez, Ph.D.
Nova Southeastern University, Florida
Vesna Ostertag, Ed.D.
Nova Southeastern University, Florida

Teaching Young Children in Multicultural Classrooms is a comprehensive study of the historical, theoretical and practical aspects of multicultural education as it relates to young children. This book includes comprehensive current and future trends, and provides many practical classroom ideas.

TABLE OF CONTENTS:
Facing the Reality of Diversity: The Intricate Nature of Our Society. The Nature of Culture, The Nature of People. Families in Our Classrooms: Many Ways, Many Voices. Who is the Child? Developmental Characteristics of Young Children. Everything Started When.....Tracing the Beginnings of Multicultural Education. Approaches to Multicultural Education: Ways & Designs for Classroom Implementation. The Classroom, Where Words Become Action. Preparing to Bring Ideas into Action. Activities & Resources for Multicultural Teaching: A World of Possibilities! A World of Resources: Involving Parents, Friends, & the Community. Appendix.

416pp., softcover, 8" x 9 1/4"
Text 0-8273-7275-2
Instructor's Manual 0-8273-7276-0

Early Childhood Curriculum: A Child's Connection to the World

Hilda Jackman, Professor Emerita
Brookhaven College, Dallas County Community College, Texas

This innovative text presents developmentally appropriate early education curriculum in a clear easy-to-read style. All chapters of the text stand alone, while complementing each other to form the whole curriculum for children from infancy to eight years. The text includes original songs, poems, dramatic play activities, as well as numerous illustrations, photos, diagrams, references, and teachers' resources.

TABLE OF CONTENTS:
PART 1: Creating the Environment That Supports Curriculum & Connects Children: STARTING THE PROCESS: CREATING CURRICULUM: PART 2: Discovering & Expanding the Early Education Curriculum: LANGUAGE & LITERACY: LITERATURE: PUPPETS: DRAMATIC PLAY & CREATIVE DRAMATICS: ARTS: SENSORY CENTERS: MUSIC & MOVEMENT: MATH: SCIENCE: SOCIAL STUDIES: APPENDICES: GLOSSARY: INDEX.

368 pp., softcover, 8 1/2" x 11"
Text 0-8273-7327-9
Instructor's Guide 0-8273-7328-7

Growing Artists: Teaching Art to Young Children

Joan Bouza Koster
Broome Community College, New York

Growing Artists will prepare pre-service teachers to teach art to children ranging from one and a half through eight years old. Each chapter focuses on a particular topic in art education, including current theory and research, the role of the teacher, how children develop artistically, creating an aesthetic environment, and integrating art into the curriculum.

TABLE OF CONTENTS:
Growing Young Artists. The Artist Inside. How Young Artists Grow. A Place For Art. Making Connections. Please Don't Eat The Art! I'm Creative. Anyone Can Walk On The Ceiling. It's A Mola. Growing Together! Caring & Sharing. Have We Grown? Appendices. References. Index.

448 pp., softcover, 8 1/2" x 11"
Text 0-8273-7544-1
Instructor's Manual 0-8273-7545-X

Student Teaching: Early Childhood Practicum Guide, 3E

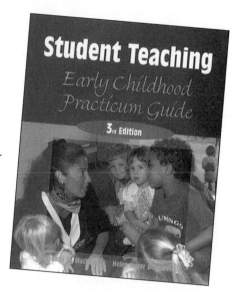

Jeanne M. Machado, Emerita, San Jose City College, California
Helen Meyer-Botnarescue, Ph.D.
California State University at Hayward

Student Teaching covers all aspects of teaching from understanding children and staff communication to relationships with parents. This book includes the characteristics of contemporary American families through multicultural and ethnic diversity. Contains chapters on dealing with children with special needs, infant and toddler placement, professionalism, trends, and issues in education.

TABLE OF CONTENTS:
ORIENTATION TO STUDENT TEACHING. Introduction to Student Teaching Practicum. Placement - First Days on the Teaching Team. A Student Teacher's Values. PROGRAMMING. Review of Child Development & Learning Theory. Activity Planning. Instruction - Group Times, Themes, & Discovery Centers. CLASSROOM MANAGEMENT REVISITED. Classroom Management Goals & Techniques. Analyzing Behavior to Promote Self-Control. COMMUNICATION. Common Problems of Student Teachers. Problem Solving. THE CHILD. Case Studies, Analysis, & Applications. Working with Children with Disabilities. PARENTS. The Changing American Family. Parents & Student Teachers. KNOWING YOURSELF & YOUR COMPETENCIES. Being Observed. Teaching Styles & Techniques. The Whole Teacher - Knowing Your Competencies. PROFESSIONAL CONCERNS. Quality Programs. Professional Commitment & Growth. Trends & Issues. INFANT/TODDLER PLACEMENT. Student Teaching with Infants & Toddlers. APPENDIX. GLOSSARY. INDEX.

464 pp., softcover , 8" x 9 1/4"
Text 0-8273-7619-7   Instructor's Guide 0-8273-7620-0

Building Understanding Together: A Constructivist Approach to Early Childhood Education

Sandra Waite-Stupiansky, Ph.D.
Edinboro University of Pennsylvania

Based on sound learning, *Building Understanding Together: A Constructivist Approach to Early Childhood Education* demonstrates the basic tenets of Piaget's constructivist theory in a comprehensive format. This text shows how constructivism can be applied to all areas of the curriculum; language arts, science, math, social studies, and the arts.

TABLE OF CONTENTS:
Understanding Constructivism. Children's Social Understandings. Guiding Children's Moral Development. Play & Learning. Young Readers & Writers. Making Math Meaningful for Young Children. Becoming Scientists. The Arts—Basic In a Constructivist Curriculum. Putting It All Together. Epilogue.

210 pp., softcover, 6" x 9"
Text 0-8273-6835-6   Instructor's Guide 0-8273-6836-4

Week by Week: Plans for Observing and Recording Young Children

Barbara Ann Nilsen, Ed.D.
Broome Community College, New York

This well-organized book provides students with a systematic plan for week-by-week documentation of each child's development in an early childhood setting. It presents instruction in the most common recording techniques as well as a review of basic child development principles. By following the week-by-week plan, the observer is able to collect periodic and useful information from a variety of sources. Diagrams, thinking exercises, and case-studies help the content meet the individual learning styles of the readers and the weekly assignments provide manageable collection of data to form a portfolio illustrating the child's development in all areas.

TABLE OF CONTENTS:

416 pp., softcover, 8 1/2" x 11"
Text 0-8273-7646-4
Instructor's Guide 0-8273-7647-2

Other Favorites Available from Delmar!

474 Science Activities for Young Children,
Green, 0-8273-6663-9

Administration of School for Young Children,
Click, 0-8273-5876-8

*Art and Creative Development for Young
Children, 2E,* Schirrmacher, 0-8273-5776-1

Assessing Young Children, Mindes, Ireton, and
Mardell-Czudnowski, 0-8273-6211-0

*Beginnings and Beyond: Foundations in Early
Childhood Education, 4E,*
Gordon & Browne, 0-8273-7271-X

Creative Activities for Young Children, 5E,
Mayesky, 0-8273-5886-5

*Creative Resources for the Early Childhood
Classroom, 2E,* Herr & Libby, 0-8273-5871-7

*Developing and Administering a Child Care
Center, 3E,* Sciarra & Dorsey, 0-8273-5875-4

*The Developmentally Appropriate Inclusive
Classroom in Early Education,*
Miller, 0-8273-6704-X

Developmentally Appropriate Practice,
Gestwicki, 0-8273-7218-3

Developmental Profiles: Prebirth to Eight, 2E,
Allen & Marotz, 0-8273-6321-4

*Early Childhood Curriculum: From
Developmental Model to Application,*
Essa & Rogers, 0-8273-7483-6

*Early Childhood Experience in Language Arts:
Emerging Literacy, 5E,*
Machado, 0-8273-5242-5

*Emergent Literacy and Dramatic Play in
Early Education,* Davidson, 0-8273-5721-4

*The Exceptional Child. Inclusion in Early
Childhood Education, 3E,*
Allen, 0-8273-6698-1

Experiences in Math for Young Children, 3E,
Charlesworth, 0-8273-7226-4

*Experiences in Movement with Music,
Activities and Theory,* Pica, 0-8273-6478-4

*Exploring Science in Early Childhood: A
Developmental Approach, 2E,*
Lind, 0-8273-7309-0

Growing Up with Literature, 2E,
Sawyer & Comer, 0-8273-7228-0

A Guidance Approach to Discipline,
Gartrell, 0-8273-5520-3

*Home, School and Community Relations: A
Guide to Working with Parents, 3E,*
Gestwicki, 0-8273-7218-3

Infant and Child Care Skills,
Bassett, 0-8273-5507-6

*Infants and Toddlers: Curriculum and
Teaching, 3E,* Wilson, Watson & Watson,
0-8273-6094-0

*Integrated Language Arts for Emerging
Literacy,* Sawyer & Sawyer, 0-8273-4609-3

*Introduction to Early Childhood Education,
2E,* Essa, 0-8273-7483-6

Math and Science for Young Children, 2E,
Charlesworth & Lind, 0-8273-5869-5

The Montessori Controversy,
Chattin-McNichols, 0-8273-4517-8

Positive Child Guidance, 2E, Miller,
0-8273-5878-4

*Practical Guide to Solving Preschool
Behavior Problems, 3E,* Essa, 0-8273-5812-1

Science Is Fun!, Oppenheim, 0-8273-7336-8

*Stories: Children's Literature in Early
Education,* Raines & Isbell, 0-8273-5509-2

Topical Child Development, Berns,
0-8273-5727-3

Understanding Child Development, 4E,
Charlesworth, 0-8273-7332-5

To Order Call Toll Free
1-800-354-9706
Fax: 1-800-487-8488
or use the Order Form on the
last page of this book.